SYBIL LE BROCQUY

CADENUS

A reassessment in the light of new evidence of the relationships between

SWIFT, STELLA *and* VANESSA

Dublin

THE DOLMEN PRESS

Printed and published at the Dolmen Press,
23 Upper Mount Street, Dublin 2,
in the Republic of Ireland.

*

Jacket and binding designed by
Louis le Brocquy RHA FSIA

*

Distributed outside Ireland by
the Oxford University Press

CO. DUBLIN
LIBRARY SERVICE
Ha
Acc. No. 132,704
Class No. 928.275
Cated. Classed
Prepared
Re-Bound £1.00
INVOICE No. 2308A

Copyright: © *Sybil Le Brocquy* 1962

To

A. Le B.

Sincere thanks are due to

The Very Reverend Dr. Armstrong, Dean of St. Patrick's, Dublin, *for permission to photograph the entry in the Cathedral Records;*
The Reverend A. Lister, *for permission to photograph the entry in the Records of the Church of St. Andrew, Northborough, England.*
Mr. P. I. King, M.A., Archivist, *Northamptonshire Record Office, England.*
Mr. G. M. Kirkwood, *Literary Department, Principal Probate Registry, Somerset House, London;*
The National Library of Ireland, *for permission to publish portion of Peter Partinton's letter;*
Miss M. Pollard, *Marsh's Library, Dublin;*
Mr. D. Englefield, M.A., *Library of the House of Commons, London;*
Louis le Brocquy
for their most generous help.

Preface

THE recent discovery of the Petition of the Van Homrigh family to "*The Right Hon*ble *the Lords Spiritual & Temporal*" and of the Judges' Opinion offered to that august body has given an opportunity for a reconsideration of the much-debated relationship between Jonathan Swift and Esther Van Homrigh.

To those critics who insist that the private life of a great writer should be left in decent obscurity, the reply must be that, in this case, there has been from the beginning no reluctance to speculate, and indeed to dogmatise freely about the ties which bound together Swift, Esther Johnson and Esther Van Homrigh.

A great deal of evidence has been given about the characters of both women; many unfavourable judgements have been passed on the younger. But, for some curious reason, Swift's own testimony about his relationship with that unhappy girl has been almost entirely ignored. The kindest picture presented has been that of a reluctant man pursued by a determined young woman, from whom he did his utmost to escape, without being too unkind to her frailty. His letters, particularly his later ones, give not the slightest support to such a theory, unless on the assumption that Swift was a hypocrite and a liar.

Such evidence as still exists in their obviously mutilated correspondence would seem to show that this extraordinary, thwarted man loved deeply, over many years, an intelligent, attractive, frustrated girl. Because no conjecture offered so far gives any plausible explanation of the tragic events which submerged Dean Swift and these two unhappy women, it is permissible to put forward yet another, in the light of new evidence.

Contents

Illustrations

I

Vanity makes terrible devastation in the female breast . . . Vanessa was exceedingly vain . . . fond of dress . . . impatient to be admired; very romantic in her turn of mind; superior in her own opinion, to all her sex: full of pertness, gaiety and pride . . . far from being either beautiful or genteel . . . happy in the thoughts of being reputed Swift's concubine, but still aiming and intending to be his wife. . . . Thus perished at Selbridge, under all the agonies of despair, Mrs. Esther Vanhomrigh, a miserable example of an ill-spent life, fantastic wit, visionary schemes and female weakness.

Remarks on the Life and Writings of Dr. J. Swift:
Orrery, 1752

I have been assured that Miss Vanhomrigh was, in her general Converse with the World, as far from encouraging any Stile of Address inconsistent with the Rules of Honour and Good-breeding as any Woman alive. Neither can it be said, if any Conclusions can be drawn from her Appearance and Behaviour in Ireland, that she was either a vain Woman or fond of Dress . . . . Her only Misfortune was that she had a Passion for Doctor Swift. Thus died at Celbridge, worthy of a happier Fate, the celebrated Mrs. Esther Vanhomrigh, a Martyr to Love and Constancy.

An Essay upon the Life, Writings and Character of Dr. Jonathan Swift: Deane Swift, 1755.*

**Deane Swift was a first cousin once removed of Jonathan Swift.*

Leabharlanna Átha Cliath

TO these two very different descriptions of Esther Van Homrigh must be added a third, from a person who, over many years, knew her far better than anyone else:

Il n'y a point de merite, ni aucun preuve de mon bon gôut, de trouver en vous tout ce que la Nature a donne á un mortel, je veux dire l'honneur, la vertue, le bon sens, l'esprit, la douceur, l'agrement et la fermité d'ame. Mais en vous cachant comme vous faites, le monde ne vous connait pas, et vous perdez l'eloge des millions de gens. Depuis que j'avois l'honneur de vous connoitre, j'ay toujours remarquè que, ni en conversation particuliere ni en general, aucun mot a eschappè de votre bouche, qui pouvoit etre mieux exprimé; et je vous jure qu'en faisant la plus severe critique, je ne pouvois jamais trouver aucun defaut, ni en vos actions ni en vos paroles. La coquetrie, l'affectation, la pruderie sont des imperfections que vous n'avez jamais connu. Et, avec tout cela, croyez vous qu'il est possible de ne vous estimer au dessus du reste du genre humain? Quelle bestes en juppes sont les plus excellentes de celles que je vois semèes dans le monde au prix de vous. En les voyant, en les entendant, je dis cent fois le jour, Ne parle, ne regarde, ne pense, ne fait rien comme ces miserables. Sont ce du meme sexe, du meme espece de creatures? Quelle cruautè, de faire mepriser, autant de gens, qui sans songer de vous seroient assès supportable.

When Jonathan Swift wrote these words to *Madam Hester Vanhumri*, on the 12th May 1719, he had known her intimately for at least eleven years; neither Lord Orrery nor Deane Swift had ever met her.

How well did Swift know this young woman, whom he could assure, after many years of acquaintance, that her perfections made all other women appear, by contrast, as *brutes in petticoats*? The answer to that question is clearly given in the letters they wrote to one another. Their story begins in 1707.

When the Rev. Dr. Swift was travelling from Dublin to London, in December 1707, he broke the tiresome journey in an inn at Dunstable, and there he almost certainly met Mrs. Van Homrigh who, with her young family, was also on her way to London, having decided that the social life of that great capital offered greater advantages than the smaller one of Dublin. She was a pleasant, irresponsible, light-hearted woman, the youngish widow of Bartholomew Van Homrigh, a Dutch gentleman who had come to Dublin from Amsterdam some time before the Revolution of 1687. How long before is not known, but it must have been a considerable time for him to have acquired the Freedom of Dublin and to have become an important citizen by 1685, when his name appears as a member of the Dublin Corporation and one of a small group appointed to supervise the building of the Tholsel. By 1688, he had become an Alderman, and his infant daughter, Esther, was therefore eligible for the Freedom of the City in the Spring of that year.

The Van Homrigh family — so they consistently spelled their name on official occasions — not unnaturally threw in their lot with the Dutch King, and fled to join his forces. In 1689, Alderman Van Homrigh *having unlawfully absented himself from the business of the City and gone to England*, was removed from the Dublin Corporation roll.

During the Revolution, Bartholomew Van Homrigh played an important part, acting as Commissary-General to the Williamite army. After King William's victory, Van Homrigh returned to Dublin, and in 1691 was reinstated as

Alderman and appointed a Sheriff of the City; later he became Chief Commissioner of Irish Revenue and Member of Parliament for Londonderry. In 1697 he was elected Lord Mayor of Dublin. During his term of office, street-lighting was first introduced there.

But for these bare outlines, little is known of this Dutch gentleman except that he was father of a famous daughter; but in 1698 he was left a small legacy by Sir William Molyneux, which bears eloquent testimony to his worth. Sir William, (who was described by the great John Locke as *that thinking gentleman, whom I am proud to call my friend*) bequeathed money for mourning rings to four only of his many close associates: the Rev. Dr. Smythe, Dean of St. Patrick's, Dublin; Bishop St. George Ashe; John Locke and Bartholomew Van Homrigh. Sir Thomas Molyneux, renowned philosopher and scientist, with his friends was responsible for the foundation of what is now the Royal Dublin Society. It would seem that Bartholomew Van Homrigh was a remarkable person, as well as being a prosperous citizen. When he died, in 1703, he was probably still a young man.

His widow was the daughter of John Stone, who like Van Homrigh had been a Commissioner of Revenue in Ireland. Lord Orrery's description of Mrs. Van Homrigh's *mean birth* is as inaccurate as his account of her daughter, Esther. Both in Dublin and in London, the Van Homrigh family moved in the higher ranks of society.

The decision to move to London was probably the result of many considerations. Mrs. Van Homrigh was extremely hospitable and fond of society; she intended sending both her sons to an English university. According to the records of Christ Church, Oxford, the elder matriculated there on the 15th April 1708, at the age of fifteen. She hoped that her well-dowered girls would make suitable marriages in London society. She may well have planned some comfortable alliance for herself — Dublin gossip had already been whispering of a romance with Sir William Robinson, her late husband's colleague. In the great world of London, opportunities for a gay life were much wider than in Ireland. The Van Homrighs were already on an excellent footing with the families of such nobility as the Marquess of Kildare, the Earl of Athlone — godfather to her son, Ginkell — and the Duke of Ormond. They would also have met visiting English notabilities at Dublin Castle, and Mrs. Van Homrigh would certainly not have forgotten the very signal honours paid to her late husband — and, possibly, to herself — during a visit to the Court of William and Mary, and also the fact that that parsimonious King had given the very considerable sum of £770 for a Mayoral chain to grace the inauguration of Bartholomew Van Homrigh as Lord Mayor of Dublin. (The gold chain with the imposing medallion was not, unfortunately, ready in time for that occasion, but has ever since lent magnificence to his successors in office). The future must have seemed very bright to Mrs. Van Homrigh as she rested in a Dunstable inn, after a very stormy passage across the Irish Sea.

That meeting of the Van Homrigh family and Dr. Swift, a poor Irish clergyman, is the first important milestone in the story of Swift and Vanessa, as young Miss Esther was to be known in the not so distant future. Five years later he wrote to her mother:

I could not see any marks in the chimney at Dunstable of the coffey Hessy spilt there.

It would seem that the stay in the Dunstable inn, long or short, was sufficient to admit Swift into a warm friendship with the family, with whom he may well have had some previous acquaintance when he was Chaplain to Lord Berkeley and to Lord Pembroke during their terms of office in

Dublin. A few weeks later, Mrs. Van Homrigh had set up her hospitable home in London, and Swift was already involved in the humorous bullying which was always so dear to him; the *Decree for concluding the Treaty between Dr. Swift and Mrs. Long,* that cousin of the Van Homrighs who was a famous Toast, and, as such, had claimed exemption from the Doctor's rule that, *all persons whatsoever shall make advances to him, as he pleases to demand.* This pleasantry, which refers to *Mrs. Van Homrigh and her fair daughter, Hessy,* purports to be the work of young Ginkell and is one of the boy's few appearances in the story.

The easy friendship between Swift and the Van Homrighs continued during his considerable stay in London. There, he was working on behalf of the Church of Ireland to obtain the remission of the First Fruits, a concession made to the Church of England, some years previously, by the Queen. After his return to Dublin in June 1709, his own records show that letters passed between himself, the mother and the elder daughter, but the letters did not survive. When he returned again to London, in September 1710, (after a short interval, during which Ginkell was dying) the Van Homrigh household rapidly became Swift's home from home. The *Journal to Stella* begins reporting dinners at *Mrs. Van's* with increasing regularity and invariable excuses — *It was such dismal weather I could not stir further,* or *out of mere listlessness, dine there often, as I did today.*

By the end of the year, Stella (Esther Johnson) in Dublin, had obviously become suspicious of danger in London, and had made some slighting reference to the Van Homrighs' social circle. To which Swift replied:

> *Sir Andrew Fountaine and I dined by invitation with Mrs. Van Homrigh. You say they are of no consequence; why they keep as good female company as I do male. I see all the drabs of quality at this end of the*

town with them. I saw the two Lady Bettys there this afternoon.

As Stella presumably knew, the two ladies were the daughter of the Duke of Ormond and the daughter of the Earl of Berkeley. Later, he cannot resist reporting to the rank-conscious Stella:

Went to Mrs. Van Homrigh's; and there was Sir Andrew Fountaine at Ombre with Lady Ashburnham, Lady Frederick Schomberg and Lady Betty Butler.

Another time he tells her that he had dined with the Van Homrighs and that later they had all gone to spend the evening with the Duchess of Ormond.

These entries offer an opportunity for some assessment of the atmosphere of the Van Homrigh home; and it may be usefully noted that Sir Andrew Fountaine, whose constant visits to that ménage are reported in the *Journal to Stella*, was a young man of considerable importance. He had graduated brilliantly at Oxford, and he was already a recognised authority on a wide range of subjects, which included Anglo-Saxon coinage, painting, porcelain and music. Sir Andrew was a wealthy young man, owner of a fine Norfolk estate, and unmarried. According to his close friend, Leibnitz, *his wit and good looks made much noise* in the European courts which he visited. He was a distinguished diplomatist, in whom Queen Anne had sufficient confidence to entrust him with a delicate mission to the court of Hanover, where her distasteful relatives waited, with ill-concealed impatience, for the throne of England.

He had probably made the acquaintance of the Van Homrigh family in Dublin some years previously, when his friend, the Earl of Pembroke, was appointed Viceroy of Ireland, and brought Sir Andrew with him in his entourage.

It is certainly a tribute to the Van Homrigh family that this distinguished young man should have become a close friend and constant visitor. The same is true of another remarkable man, Erasmus Lewis, who was also on terms of close intimacy. Like Sir Andrew, Lewis was a brilliant young man, who had spent much time travelling abroad and had served as Secretary to the Embassies in Paris and Brussels, before being appointed Under-Secretary of State under the Earl of Dartmouth. Swift made constant use of his good offices for the forwarding and receiving of letters, and he was a confidant in the Swift-Vanessa correspondence; her bequest to him in her will proves that her friendship and gratitude lasted to the very end of her life. That Erasmus Lewis, friend of Prior, Arbuthnot, Gay and Pope, was also on intimate terms with the Van Homrigh family is a tribute to them and their circle of friends. The atmosphere must have been a congenial one to have attracted, amongst others, such men as Swift, Fountaine and Lewis, as well as Charles Ford, who was described as *the best lay-scholar of his time and nation.*

As to their female friends, Swift himself tells Stella, *the drabs of quality* formed their intimate circle.

Unless one relies on the evidence of the type of people who frequented the Van Homrigh home, there is little to help any estimation of the family. Even in the case of its most famous member, the only direct evidence is that of Swift. But the abhorrence of this near-vacuum has produced much unfortunate conjecture, which has studiously ignored the plain evidence of Swift's letters to her.

At an early stage, biographers *took sides* in the implied rivalry between Stella and Vanessa, with the unfortunate result that Vanessa's denigration was regarded as essential to Stella's glorification. After Stella's death, Swift left a fairly detailed description of her character and personal appearance. All that he definitely tells about Vanessa's looks is that her eyes were *not* black.

There exist a number of portraits labelled *Esther Johnson*, or *Esther Van Homrigh;* unfortunately, there is no unanimity in the labels, nor, indeed, any certainty that either young woman is the subject of any of the pictures. One drawing of Esther Johnson exists, done by her friend Archdeacon Parnell; it appears in the Faulkner edition of Swift's works, published in Dublin in 1768, when some of her friends were still alive to confirm or repudiate its likeness. It may well be an authentic portrait, but it bears no resemblance to any of the other alleged portraits.

Of Esther Van Homrigh, there remains not even a pencil sketch which can be relied on to show what she looked like; there is not even a grave, where a tombstone might offer a silent testimony of her last resting-place. Everything seems to have conspired to hide all traces of the unhappy girl who, according to Swift, made all other women appear *like brutes in petticoats.* But *his* evidence has been almost totally ignored, or else completely mis-interpreted.

By May 1711 Swift has the use of a room of his own at *Mrs. Van's* where he keeps his *best gown and periwig to put on when I come to town and be a spark.* It must have been with very mixed feelings that Stella read:

I got little MD's letter, No. 15, *and I read it in a closet they lend me at Mrs. Van's.*

Since he had informed MD (his code name for Esther Johnson and Rebecca Dingley) that he changed his wig and gown twice daily, the ladies in Dublin must have realised that he was a constant visitor at the *Van's.*

It is very significant that Swift's garrulous *Journal to Stella* contains only three allusions to *Mrs. Van's* daughter. One such entry, dated February 1710-11, throws a melancholy shadow of future events:

Her eldest daughter is come of age and going to Ireland to look after her fortune and get it into her own hands.

The first existing letter from Swift to Esther Van Homrigh (*little Missessy*) is dated 18th December 1711. It is a covering letter for her eye alone, enclosing *a starched letter* to herself for display to her family and a long letter, which he asked Esther to forward to her cousin, Mrs. Long.

> *I have writ three or four lies in as many lines. Pray seal up this letter to Mrs. Long, and let no one read it but yourself. I suppose this packet will lie two or three hours, till you awake. And pray, let the outside starched letter to you be seen, after you have sealed that to Mrs. Long. See what art people must use, though they mean ever so well. Now are you and Puppy lying at your ease without dreaming anything of all this. Adieu, till we meet over a pot of coffee or an orange in the Sluttery, which I have so often found to be the most agreeable chamber in the world.*

In the enclosed letter to Anne Long which *Missessy* is bidden to read, he humorously lists Esther's faults, but states, *I think there is not a better girl on earth. I have a mighty friendship for her.* The *starched* letter, written to be produced for the family, no longer exists; so it is not possible to know whether the *three or four lies* appear in it, or whether the criticisms he makes of Esther in the letter to her cousin are referred to. The *starched letter* is the first of many precautions taken by Swift to guard his correspondence from prying eyes; they range from the use of cyphers to the use of Latin and his curious French.

This year is one of the greatest importance in the relationship between Swift and Esther Van Homrigh. In his *Journal to Stella* he records, on the 4th February, 1711-12:

> *I was this morning soliciting at the House of Commons' door for Mr. Vesey, a son of the Archbishop of Tuam, who petitioned for a Bill to relieve him of some difficulty about his estate. I secured him above fifty members.*

He does *not* tell Stella that, a couple of weeks previously, the Van Homrigh family had petitioned the House of Lords for a similar private bill, to enable them to dispose of their Irish estate, since

> *all the parties concerned in Interest in the same are now residing and intend to make their residence in England, and are therefore desireous that the said Premises may be sold and the Produce thereof brought into this Kingdom, which will be more beneficial for all the Parties concerned,*

to quote from the opinion of the learned judges, appointed by the Lords to advise them on the Petition.

Swift, at this time, was visiting the Van Homrigh family at least twice daily, frequenting the Sluttery, which he described as *the most agreeable chamber in the world.* On the 14th January, one week before the Petition was presented, Swift dined with Mrs. Van Homrigh and, next night, he had a very prolonged meeting with Sir William Robinson, one of the closest friends of the family, who for many years had been trying to unravel Bartholomew Van Homrigh's tangled affairs. A few weeks later, Swift records in his *Journal to Stella 7th March. I was today at the House of Lords about a friend's Bill.*

His omission of the friend's name is highly significant. It is straining all probability to believe that this influential man, who was so actively interesting himself in Mr. Vesey's private Bill, was not also doing his utmost to help his close friend, Mrs. Van Homrigh, to get a similar private Bill through the House of Lords. It is, therefore, extremely significant to read in this Petition, which is signed by the four surviving members of the family:

> *The said Ginkell is since dead, and Hester the daughter is now come to age and in prospect of marriage; but cannot receive her portion by reason the same Bartholomew, her brother, being only of the age of 19 years.*

The date of this Petition is 22nd January 1711-12. If at that time Esther Van Homrigh had any *prospect of marriage* it could only have been with Swift, who certainly advised and probably drew up the Petition for her mother. Lest there be any lingering doubt that he was intimately concerned with the proceedings, there is his letter to Esther, dated August 1722, in which he reminds her, eleven years later,

You were once a better solicitor, when you could contrive to make others desire your consent to an Act of Parliament against their own interest, to advance yours.

This Petition has been inexplicably overlooked by the host of interested persons, who have speculated about the baffling relationship between Swift and Esther Van Homrigh. It gives an entirely new starting point if it be conceded that, in the year 1711, Swift was regarded by Mrs. Van Homrigh as being betrothed to her elder daughter, who was then just under twenty-three, Swift being forty-four. Because he was extremely inaccurate about ages—and many other things—or because of the demands of rhyme, Swift immortalised this period with the lines, in *Cadenus and Vanessa*,

Vanessa, not in years a score
Dreams of a Gown of forty four.

the Right Hon.ble the Lords Spiritual & Temporal in Parliam.t Assembled

The humble Petition of Hester Vanhomrigh widdow and Relict of Bartholomew Vanhomrigh late of the City of Dublin Esq.r and Hester Vanhomrigh their daughter and Bartholomew and Mary Vanhomrigh Infants by their said Mother their Guardian

[...]eth

That your Petitioners husband and Father Bartholomew Vanhomrigh dec.d did by his last Will and Testament bearing date the 2d day of June 1701 Give and Devise That all his Lands tenements Chattles Reall and Personall Goods of all kind of Worldly Substance that he had or should have or be Intituled unto at the time of his death should within two Months after his decease be Inventoried valued and Apprised (and after his debts and ffunerall charges satisfied) should be divided into so many equall parts as he should have Children living att the time of his death and one part more to be put out to Interest which Interest he did thereby direct to be paid to your Pet.r Hester his wife during her Life with other Devises over and made his said wife Hester John Pearson and Peter Partington Executors and Overseers as in and by the said Will may more fully appear.

Your Pet.rs further shew that the said Devisor dyed some time after making his said Will leaving the said Hester his widdow, the said Hester and Mary his two daughters, and Ginkell and Bartholomew his two sons all Under the age of 21 years, and that the Will was afterwards Establisht by Decree in the High Court of Chancery in Ireland as by the said Decree relation being thereunto had may appear.

That the said Ginkell is since dead under the Age of 21 years and Hester the daughter is now come to Age, and in prospect of marriage, but cannot receive her portion by reason the said Bartholomew her Brother being only of the Age of 19 years cannot sell any part of the Devised premisses without the Aid of an Act of Parliament.

That the said Peter Partington hath ever since the death of the said Devisor taken upon him the Mannagement of the said Estate which being dispersed in severall Counties in Ireland and all the Petitioners living in this Kingdome are desirous to sell and dispose of the said Estate so left to them and bring the produce thereof into this Kingdom which will tend very much to the advantage of your Petitioners.

Therefore your Petitioners humbly pray your Lordships to permitt them to bring in a Bill to vest the Lands tenements and hereditaments of which the said Devisor died Seized in Trustees and their heirs to be sold and that the purchase money to be gott for the same may be divided into five Equall parts, One part whereof to be enjoyed by the said Hester the widdow during her life with power to dispose of five hundred pounds thereof as by the said Will is directed, and the other four parts together with what shall remaine of the said fifth part after the decease of the said Hester the widdow to be equally divided between the other Petitioners the Children of the said Bartholomew Vanhomrigh.

And your Pet.rs shall ever pray &c

E Van Homrigh
E Van Homrigh
Van Homrigh
Mary Van Homrigh

PLATE I The Van Homrigh Petition.

II

AT this point it is useful to consider the circumstances of Swift's public life, which had so much bearing upon his private world. In the portrait painted by Jervas, immediately after Swift's return to London in 1710, he sits proudly, in the splendour of *my best gown and periwig, to put on when I come to town and be a spark,* the very picture of clerical confidence and decent gravity. Indeed, the forceful dignity of the pose would merit those more lavish episcopal trimmings which Swift had then every reason to expect. His Whig friends, as he reported immediately in the Journal, *were ravished to see me, and would lay hold of me as a twig, while they are drowning.*

Politically, the Whigs *were* drowning, through the hushed, back-stairs diplomacy of the humble Mrs. Masham, who had meekly supplanted the masterful Duchess of Marlborough in Queen Anne's simple affections. Swift, thoroughly resentful of the failure of the Whig lords to obtain him any reward for his services, was now not unwilling to acknowledge in the newly victorious Tory party, the true protectors of the Church and State. The Tories had the good sense to recognise, immediately, the deadly value of Swift's pen; and so a new alliance was born and, in 1710, he had once again bright prospects of rapid preferment.

Considering the acuteness of Swift's judgement in most things, it is a mystery that he apparently never realised until the very end that, whether Whig or Tory were in power, he was completely barred from any clerical appointment which required the Queen's consent. His early masterpiece, *The Tale of a Tub,* had profoundly shocked Queen Anne, one of whose characteristics was a deep and very genuine piety, combined with a dogged devotion to the Church of England. Theologically, she was her father's daughter, in reverse; where he was fanatically devoted to the Church of Rome, she was equally dedicated to the Church of England. Anyone who could treat that Church with irreverent levity, as Swift had done, was a blasphemer, or an atheist and totally unfitted for clerical office. Indeed, Queen Anne carried her convictions so far that, in spite of her passion for listening to sermons, she never once permitted that very distinguished clergyman to preach before her. Over years, Swift haunted the Court—at St. James, Windsor, Kensington, Richmond—where he was on intimate terms of friendship with the most powerful men and women surrounding the Queen; but his friends were never sufficiently powerful to overcome the Queen's distaste, and Swift was never permitted to make his bow to her. Since Queen Anne held all important clerical appointments firmly in her poor, gouty hands, Swift's chances of preferment were negligible, although he could not or would not recognise that unpalatable fact.

To return to January 1711-12, when the Van Homrigh Petition was drafted, Swift was almost at the peak of his career, the object of flattery, both social and political. He was, it is true, often hard-up, but money could always be borrowed by a man of his position so apparently marked out for imminent preferment. He and his Irish serving-man moved lodgings fairly frequently; he was a welcome visitor at the dining tables of the great and boasted that he scarcely ever had a meal at home. He had also the use of a room in Mrs. Van Homrigh's ever-hospitable establishment, presumably that *Sluttery, which I have so often found to be the most agreeable Chamber in the World*, where he savoured *Mishessy's* sugared oranges and coffee. But for increasing *giddy spells* and a deafness in his left ear (which he shared with his good friend the Lord Treasurer), all was exceedingly well with Dr. Jonathan Swift.

Mrs. Van Homrigh's affairs were not nearly so satisfactory, although there is no reason to suppose that she confided the full extent of her embarrassments to her good friend, the Doctor. Already, on 5th October 1709, her finances were in a precarious condition. In a letter of that date from Peter Partinton,[1] one of the co-executors of her husband's will, he refuses to honour a bill she has drawn for £100, and he begs her to curtail her expenditure. It was a *cri du coeur* across the Irish Sea:

Where this money is to be found, God Almighty only knows. If you doe, for God's sake, in your next tell me and upon the Worde of a Christian, noe Stone shall be left unturned nor noe Pains thought too much to serve you and yours. Could you sende me a Pattent to coyne Money and Bullion enough, I would sitt up Night and Day to serve you. But since you cannot doe it, you must not expect I will throw myself in Jayl for another's Debt.

That Mrs. Van Homrigh should find herself in trouble after a couple of years in London society is not surprising, if it be remembered that her husband's estate had been left in great confusion at his death and that his affairs were still unsettled. What is much more surprising is to find that her sons, Ginkell and Bartholomew—aged, respectively, about fifteen and sixteen—were in considerable trouble, financial and otherwise. In the same letter, Mr. Partinton writes:

I am exceedingly concerned at the Relation you give about Mr. Ginkell and his late proceedings. I pray God Almighty to open his eyes and convince him of the Wrong he has both done himself and the Reflections he has caste upon the whole Family.

(Whatever Mr. Ginkell's *late proceedings* may have been, he had little time left to *caste Reflections* upon himself or the Family; according to the burial register of St. James's

---

[1] A.L.S. National Library of Ireland.

Church, London, *Gingell Van Homeridge Gent* was buried there on 8th October, 1710, almost exactly a year later.) Mr. Partinton adds:

> *You may depende upon it, Mr. Barty's Crime is an extraordinary Waisting of Money occationed by keeping bad Company and striving to imitate others that are far above him . . . . . I find all Persons gives mee the deafe Ear, Mr. Ginkell nor Mr. Barty will not confine themselves within their allowance that is judged sufficient to them and Madm. Van Homrigh still goes along the olde Roade, never considering the Reckoning at last that must be made.*

Mr. Partinton ends by protesting his extreme, and, under the circumstances, not unnatural anxiety to be finished with the Van Homrigh business affairs. Yet, fourteen years later, when Esther died, he was still deeply involved. Later still, her heirs, Dr. Berkeley and Mr. Marshall, were vainly struggling to wind up the Van Homrigh estate, which Mr. Partinton had been handling for nearly quarter of a century. As an executor, he would appear to have been very unlucky, over-conscientious, or extremely incompetent. Nor did the difficulties die with him. In a letter from Dr. Berkeley to Mr. Prior, dated 1725, he implores:

> *In God's sake adjust, finish, conclude anyway with Partinton; for at the rate we have gone on these two years, we may go on twenty*!

Evidently Mr. Partinton junior was as difficult to deal with as his late father had been.

The picture of Mrs. Van Homrigh which emerges from Mr. Partinton's despairing letter gives little hope of any real reformation and so, a couple of years later, he is found agreeing to the petition of the family to *the Right Hon.ble the Lords Spiritual and Temporal in Parliament assembled* for a Private Bill, to enable them to dispose of their properties which *lye dispersed in several Counties of the Kingdom of Ireland*.

It is an interesting sidelight on the times that the original will of Bartholomew Van Homrigh could not safely be sent from Dublin *by reason of the danger of the Seas,* and Mr. Partinton had to send a certified copy to the House of Lords in London. This copy, unfortunately, cannot now be traced, and the original will was destroyed, with so many other valuable documents, in the holocaust of the Record Office in Dublin in 1922.

Whether any of their Irish property was actually realised, after the English House of Lords passed the Bill, it is not possible to discover. Certainly, the fine mansion at Celbridge and the Dublin house in Turnstile Alley were still owned by Esther during her lifetime. Her brother, Bartholomew, died in 1715 in his property in Co. Cork.

There is no way of knowing how much Swift really knew about the Van Homrighs' affairs when the Petition was being drawn up. On paper, the property was impressive. Bartholomew Van Homrigh's estate is variously estimated up to £20,000. According to Betham's Genealogical Abstracts, each daughter became entitled to £250 a year, on attaining majority or on marriage. Ginkell was already dead in 1711, when the Petition to the House of Lords was drawn up, so, according to the will, the estate was to be divided into four parts, the widow having a life interest in one part. She was also given power to bequeath £500 of the capital as she wished. This power she duly exercised in her will, put into probate in February 1713-14—a document which also seems to have escaped notice.

It would appear then that the two Van Homrigh daughters and their brother would be entitled to about £5,000 apiece, if the property could be realised; they would also be entitled to share the further £5,000 on Mrs. Van Homrigh's death. (Mrs. Van Homrigh died early in 1713-14, Barthlomew died in 1715, leaving his estate to his sisters for their lives. Mary Van Homrigh died in 1720, bequeathing everything to Esther, so that—in theory—she was mistress of the entire Van Homrigh fortune at her death in 1723.)

In 1711, the value of money was enormously higher than today. Swift's mother is said to have lived *and wanted for nothing* on an annuity of £20. Swift, in his Journal, records the difficulty his cousin had in living on £18 a year. So that Esther Van Homrigh, either with an income of £250 a year, or a fortune of £5,000, was a reasonably wealthy young woman, sufficiently well endowed to be a suitable wife for a prospective Dean, or even a Bishop, in England.

The two significant words are *prospective* and *England.* Swift was a man with an overweening sense of his own dignity and independence, fostered, perhaps, by his years of dependence and enforced humility as a member of Sir William Temple's household. Under no circumstances would he have consented to figure as the poor suitor of a rich girl; he would certainly have insisted that the betrothal be kept absolutely secret between Esther, her mother and himself until such a time as he had been appointed to his Deanery or Bishopric, in England. But England it had to be; firstly, because to Swift England was home and Ireland bitter exile, and secondly, because *the Ladies* were living in Dublin.

III

THE Ladies, Esther Johnson and Rebecca Dingley, (both by eighteenth century usage enjoying an honorary *Mrs.*) were two Englishwomen, whom Swift had encouraged to come to live near him in Dublin in 1701, some ten years previously. Esther had then been about twenty and her companion some fifteen years older.

Both during her lifetime and afterwards, gossip persistently whispered that Esther Johnson was the illegitimate child of Sir William Temple; and rumour was considerably stimulated when, at his death, he left her land in Ireland worth more than £1,000. The fact that she is described in the will as *servant of my sister Giffard* may well have been an embarrassment to her, but did nothing to allay gossip. Sir William also left £20 to her widowed mother, who had been, and remained for many years, a serving-woman to Lady Giffard, who was virtual head of her brother's household at Moor Park. When the Temple household there was broken up by Sir William Temple's death, Esther Johnson, on Swift's advice, arrived in Dublin accompanied by Rebecca Dingley. As Denis Johnston points out in his penetrating and excellent study, *In Search of Swift*, it is very curious that this other lady, who was a close relative of the Temples, should have been willing to come to Ireland as an attendant-chaperone to the child of her cousin's serving-woman.

Many years later, immediately after Esther Johnson's death, Swift wrote a moving description of her many excellences: her kindness, her courage, her beauty, her wit. During her lifetime we get glimpses of her character in the poems he wrote and the allusions to her in letters. But the clearest picture of these two women and their relationship to Swift is found in the misnamed *Journal to Stella*, which covers the years he spent in London between September 1710 and June 1713. Over most of those years, he wrote almost daily, reporting his private and public activities, his hopes and fears, his illnesses, almost everything which concerned him—with one notable exception. Only once does he actually refer to Esther Johnson's namesake, Esther Van Homrigh.

About this time, Swift wrote the much discussed poem [1]*Cadenus & Vanessa*, and it will be convenient to anticipate its appearance and to refer to this second Esther, from now on, by the name he then gave her, and under which she has reached a tragic fame.

When Thomas Sheridan in 1784 edited the *Journal*, the letters appeared for the first time consecutively and in correct order. But, by giving a misleading title, he helped to deepen the mystery of Swift's relationship to Esther Johnson. It is, therefore, important to remember that, in no sense were they love letters, written to *Stella*—for the greater number were addressed to Mrs. Dingley and the contents were invariably intended to be read by both ladies. The name *Stella* was not used by Swift until nine years later. The Ladies, in reply, wrote joint letters to Swift. Every letter he wrote was addressed to MD, and Swift very clearly explains the initials:

> 18*th Feb.* 1710-11 . . . . *certain ladies of Presto's acquaintance* . . . . . *are called, in a certain language, our little MD.*

The exact significance of the initials is a matter for speculation, but *my dears* has been suggested. Occasionally the initials DD appear, which may well stand for *dear Dingley;* sometimes *ppt* refers to Esther, and it has been suggested, may represent *poppet*, a popular term of endearment. The use of *Presto* for PDFR is another change made by the first editor. Presto was a name given to Swift by the Italian Duchess of Shrewsbury, who couldn't manage the English version.

[1] See Appendix IX, page 156.

Again, there has been much guesswork as to the significance of PDFR, and some agreement that it stands for *poor dear foolish rogue.* Like the *little language* which Swift often makes use of in the letters, no certain translation is now possible. Occasionally, he combines all three in PMD, as in the following:

> *I believe there has not been one moment since we parted, wherein a letter was not upon the road, going or coming, to or from PMD. If the Queen knew, she would give us a pension; for we bring good luck to their post-boys and their packet.*

His own explanation of the *Journal* is given later on:

> *23rd October* 1710 . . . . . *I know it is neither wit nor diversion to tell you every day where I dine, neither do I write it to fill my letter; but I fancy I shall, some time or other, have the curiosity of seeing some particulars how I passed my life, when I was absent from MD this time . . . . I am weary of friends, and friendships are all monsters but MD's.*

One of the many odd circumstances in the relation of Swift and these two women—now aged thirty and fortyfive—is that he took such extraordinary precautions never, so far as is known, to see either of them alone. He would seem to have carried this so far as never to have written them anything except a joint letter. The *Journal* is full of passages such as:

> *I wish my dearest pretty Dingley and Stella a happy New Year.*
> *Goodnight my own two dearest MD.*
> *January 16th* 1710-11. *Farewell, dearest beloved MD, and love from Presto, who has not had one happy day since he left you, as hope saved. It is the last sally I will ever make, but I hope it will turn to some account. I have done more for these, and I think they are more honest than the*

last, however, I will not be disappointed. I would make MD and me easy, and I never desired more.

The *they* above refers to his new friends in the Tory party who, he hoped, would prove *more honest* in rewarding his political services than the Whigs had been. It is informative to expand the initials, so that the sentence reads—

I would make Esther Johnson, Rebecca Dingley and me easy, and I never desired more.

Again, soon after he writes:

My new friends are very kind and I have promises enough but I do not count on them . . . . . However, we will see what may be done, and, if nothing at all, I shall not be disappointed; although perhaps MD may, and then I shall be sorrier for their sakes than my own.

The stress is always on his desire to make their circumstances easier. He was already making them an annual allowance. Had his letters protested his desire to improve the circumstances of either lady, it might have been construed into matrimonial intentions; but since both were always linked in any future prospects, he was perfectly safe. So far as Esther Johnson was concerned, on paper or off, Swift was invariably the soul of discretion.

What then was his attitude towards this young woman whom he had known intimately since he taught little Esther Johnson her early lessons at Moor Park? Years later, Swift wrote these lines to her:

Thou, Stella, wert no longer young
When first my harp for thee was strung
Without one word of Cupid's darts,
Of killing eyes, or bleeding hearts;
With friendship and esteem possest
I ne'er admitted Love a guest.

Into the company of *friendship and esteem*, he may never have admitted *Love*, in the usual sense of the word, but it is impossible to read the *Journal* without becoming aware of the deep affection which warms it. Swift's attitude is that of an extremely affectionate, rather humorous uncle towards a favourite and favoured niece. The letters are full of loving banter, *saucy jades, lazy sluttikins, blundering goose-caps, dearest sauce-faces.* He constantly corrects her spelling blunders—sixteen in one letter—twits her about the Dublin circle of card-playing nonentities; he scolds her for forgetting his messages; boasts of his personal successes, of his familiarity with the great. He addresses the pair, oddly, as *Sirrahs, lads, dear brave boys.* He does little shopping commissions for them in London, buys spectacles, chocolate, tobacco for snuff, aprons, tea. He reports on the weather:

5th October 1711. *To-day it grows bloody cold.*

But, above all, and in almost every letter, he is concerned about Esther Johnson's health. After her death, he wrote:

> *She was sickly from childhood to about fifteen, when she grew into perfect health.*

She certainly did not enjoy perfect health during the years 1710-1713. The symptoms of her illness recur so frequently in the *Journal* that it is of interest to list some of them. A few weeks after his arrival in London he writes:

> *3rd October* 1710. *This morning Stella's sister came to see me . . . she gave me a bottle of palsy-water and desired that I would send it by the first convenience . . . She promises a quart bottle of the same.*

A fortnight later:

> *I got MD's fourth letter, at the Coffee-house today. God Almighty bless poor Stella and her eyes and head. What shall we do to cure them, poor dear life? Your disorders*

are a pull-back for your good qualities. Would to Heaven I were this minute shaving your poor dear head, either here or there. Pray do not write, nor read this letter, nor anything else.

And a few weeks later:

I saw your mother and made her give me a pint of palsy-water . . . and sent it to Mr. Smith, who goes tomorrow for Ireland.
Poor Stella's eyes. God bless them and send them better. Pray spare them.

Months later:

Is Stella well enough to go to Church, pray? No numbing left? No darkness in your eyes?

A year later he remarks:

I hoped Stella would have done with her illness but I think we both have the faculty never to part with a disorder for ever.

Meanwhile, the Ladies tried that great Eighteenth century cure-all, the Spa, and had drunk the waters at Wexford and Templeoge, as well as making many country visits in search of better health. Swift writes to them to Wexford:

Don't think of reading or writing until your eyes are well, and long well. God be thanked the ugly numbing is gone . . . Why do you write, Sirrah Stella, when you find your eyes so weak that you cannot see?

And, finally, when in February 1712 he is developing shingles in London, he writes:

The pain has left my shoulder and crept to my neck and collar-bone. It makes me think of poor Stella's blade-bone . . . dogs gnawing.

Shortly after his arrival in London he records:

Sir Andrew Fountaine has been very ill . . . The nurse

asked me whether I thought it possible he could live, for the doctors said not. I said I believed that he would live; for I found the seeds of life in him, which I observe seldom fail. And I found them in poor dearest Stella, when she was ill many years ago.

This, presumably, was the serious illness which Swift says she suffered before she was fifteen, and of which it seems she had nearly died. It is tempting to diagnose that illness from her reported symptoms — severe headaches, constant eye trouble, numbness and acute pain in her neck and shoulder. All these symptons are associated with the after-effects of a facial palsy which with eighteenth century treatments would almost certainly leave behind such long-lasting disabilities.

So that Esther Johnson, living a quiet life in Dublin's Cathedral world, a delicate woman in her early thirties, may well have suffered too from the growing certainty that Swift was in constant contact with a vital, attractive young lady, many years her junior, who inhabited the gay world of London. *The danger of the seas* might interfere with the safe passage of Bartholomew Van Homrigh's will, but it certainly would not stop the passage of gossip between London and Dublin. Apart from Swift's treasured and warmly affectionate relationship with Esther Johnson, (a relationship which obviously quite gladly included her friend and companion Rebecca Dingley) and his knowledge that his marriage with another woman would have disastrous reactions on that relationship, it must also have been obvious to him that the consequences of such a marriage would be extremely damaging to himself, in Ireland.

When first the Ladies came to make their home in Dublin, as Swift relates, their appearance was highly suspect in that social group which revolved around the two Cathedrals. (Dublin is probably the only city which, for curious reasons, has two Protestant Cathedrals within a stone's throw of one another.) But their circumspect and exemplary behaviour gradually won them a very high place in the affectionate regard of the host of Anglo-Irish divines who filled the leading clerical positions in eighteenth century Dublin; and the Ladies were also welcome guests in the homes of some of the leading citizens. For more than ten years, those friends had taken it more or less for granted that Doctor Swift, in his own good time and when his income warranted it, would marry the charming young woman, whom he had persuaded to come to live in Dublin. Ranged behind the claims of Esther Johnson was a very solid group who, from the Archbishop of Dublin down, would have been scandalised at any suggestion that Swift would marry anyone else. All hope of Irish promotion would, at the very least, have been seriously jeopardised and many of his friendships would have been broken. Had Swift wished to marry in Ireland, he had only one choice: the pleasant young woman who had waited, in patient dignity, for ten years.

So that if Swift *had* proposed marriage to Vanessa he must have done so in the certainty that, henceforth, his living was to be in England. He may well have indulged in wishful thinking, to blur the outlines of an unpleasant picture. Ambition is a conjurer that can produce almost limitless *rabbits* to suit the Act, and Swift was an extremely ambitious man. With greater revenues at his disposal (he may well have reasoned) he could make a far larger allowance to *dearest MD*, so making their lives more easeful . . . . After all, they had obviously learned to live very pleasantly without him, owing to his lengthy absence from Dublin . . . There would, undoubtedly, be a painful interlude, but there was no real reason why the old, affectionate correspondence should not eventually be re-established between Dublin and London . . . And, if not, a powerful Churchman, living in England among his own peers, would find eventual compensation for the loss of the old affection in the new, passionate devotion of a most attractive, well-dowered young wife . . .

Swift must have been well aware that there was no possibility of the Ladies returning to England. Like so many English people, they had become *more Irish than the Irish themselves.* As Swift tells us, Stella *loved Ireland much better than the generality of those who owe both their birth and riches to it.* There was also the important consideration that, whereas in Ireland Esther Johnson had won for herself a very definite and dignified place in a pleasant society, in her native England she was at a serious social disadvantage. Her mother was still a serving-woman, employed in Lady Giffard's household at £12 a year; her only sister was married to a man who could do no better, with Swift's influence behind him, than a lowly job in the Salt Office, with a salary of £40. Esther Johnson's only social asset in England was the doubtful one of her rumoured illegitimate connection with the Temple family. So that in 1711 there was no question of her returning to London; and at that time there seemed even less chance that Vanessa would ever leave it for Ireland. The scene was set and the choice was Swift's. He was the uneasy base of a triangle whose sides were equal and opposite.

IV

AT the end of March 1712, Swift had a very severe attack of shingles, and he describes the agonies he endured in great detail in the *Journal*. Swift was a very sick man, and it was several months before he had completely recovered. The kindly Mrs. Van Homrigh and her family would have been assiduous in their attentions to the suffering man, and may well have moved him to their own lodgings. Severe shingles is not a disease to be borne in solitude. About this time, too, Swift seems to have dismissed his servant, Patrick, whom he had brought from Dublin and who was devoted to Mrs. Dingley. It is significant, too, that at this time, the daily *Journal* to MD ceases. Occasional letters, with long intervals, took its place. Perhaps Swift's conscience smote him when he wrote, on 15th Sept. 1712, after an interval of five weeks:

> *I was never so long without writing to MD as now since I left them, nor ever will again while I am able to write.*

The letter ends:

> *Love PDFR who loves MD above all things. Farewell dearest, ten thousand times dearest MD.*

But there is another interval of three weeks until the next letter, and the long gaps continue. The Ladies must have wondered . . .

On 1st August, 1712, just six months after the Petition had been presented and a couple of months after the private Bill had been passed, Swift wrote the second existing letter to Vanessa. He writes from Windsor, where he has been staying:

. . . . I am so weary of this place that I am resolved to leave it in two days, and not return in three weeks. I will come as early on Monday as I can find opportunity and will take a little Grubstreet lodging, pretty near where I did before and dine with you thrice a week; and will tell you a thousand secrets, provided you will have no quarrels with me. Don't remember me to Moll, but humble service to your Mother.

Moll, of whom the jocose remark is made, was Vanessa's delicate fifteen-year old sister, Mary, to whom Swift used to *tell stories and bring sugar-plums.* Presumably he made his visit to London, as the next letter, written from Windsor suggests that the Van Homrigh family visit that town:

. . . . for four or five days. Five pounds will maintain you and pay your coach backwards and forwards . . . . I will steal to town, one of these days, and catch you napping. I desire you and Moll will walk as often as you can in the Park, and do not sit moping at home, so that you can neither work nor read, nor play, nor care for company. I long to drink a dish of coffee in the Sluttery, and hear you dun me for secrets and: Drink your coffee—why don't you drink your coffee?

Ten years later, Swift was still reproaching her for moping and lack of social interests. In his absence, life stood still for Vanessa.

Soon after, Swift is back in London, and there is no need for further letters since he was presumably, according to his promise, dining with the Van Homrighs *thrice a week* and relaxing in the pleasant atmosphere of the Sluttery, which he had *so often found to be the most agreeable chamber in the world.*

The political whirlpool, of which Queen Anne's court was the muddy vortex, is not of importance here, except in so far as it affected the private life of Swift. The ever-widening rift between the Tory leaders, which Swift worked so feverishly to mend, made it tragically obvious that their Ministry could not possibly survive much longer. The nation's uneasiness about the childless Queen's failing health—public Funds rose or fell with every new batch of rumours—was enormously increased by the uncertainty of the Succession. English eyes were fixed, in hope or fear, on the unsavoury Court in Hanover, or on the romantic Stuarts in their sad, shabby exile. Never a strong woman, Queen Anne's health was obviously declining rapidly. Rumour buzzed like a bluebottle fly. Swift records in the *Journal* on 9th October 1712:

I asked . . . . . Lady Masham, seriously whether the Queen were at all inclined to dropsy . . . . She assured me that she was not. So did her physician, Arbuthnot, who always attends her. Yet these devils have spread that she has holes in her legs and runs at her navel and I know not what.

Nevertheless, Swift must have realised that the reign was drawing to a close; that the Tory Ministry was fast losing its cohesion and therefore its power; and that he, himself, through his political activities, had made so many bitter enemies amongst his former friends, the Whigs, that with the fall of the Tories he would lose all chance of preferment and, very possibly, his liberty itself. During the previous year, various English Bishoprics and Deaneries had been awarded to him—by rumour. In cold fact, Swift was still the same poor rector of a poor Irish parish, who had arrived in London in 1710.

In the middle of April 1713, the omission of his name from a new list of clerical appointments brought things to a head. On 13th April, he writes in the *Journal*:

I bid Mr. Lewis tell the Lord Treasurer that I take nothing ill of him but his not giving me timely notice, as he had promised to do, if he found the Queen would do nothing for me . . . . I told the Lord Treasurer I had nothing to do but go to Ireland immediately, for I could not, with any reputation, stay longer here, unless I had something honourable immediately given me . . . . . I told the Duke of Ormond my intentions. He is content Sterne should be a Bishop, and I have St. Patrick's.

The Queen's closest friend, Lady Masham, wept openly at the prospect of losing him to faraway Dublin, and did her utmost to persuade her royal mistress to make Swift a Prebend of Windsor. But Anne remained adamant. She probably salved her conscience for Swift's appointment as Dean of St. Patrick's, by the fact that that Deanery was in the gift of the Duke of Ormond.

Swift was deeply humiliated by the whole transaction.

The Lord Treasurer said he would not be satisfied, but that I must be a prebendary of Windsor. Thus he perplexes things . . . . I confess, as much as I love England, I am so angry at this treatment that, if I had my choice, I would rather have St. Patrick's . . . . Neither can I feel joy at passing my days in Ireland; and I confess I thought the Ministry would not let me go,

he wrote to MD.

But the Tory Ministry *did* let him go, Lord Oxford and Lord Bolingbroke being too occupied with their private feuds to realise how little they could afford to lose his services, at so critical a time.

The Duke of Ormond is to send over an order, making me Dean of St. Patrick's . . . . I suppose MD is malicious enough to be glad and rather have it than Wells.

He adds, perhaps with a touch of malice himself:

They expect me to pass next Winter here.

It was then more than three months since the Ladies had written to him, as Swift had complained. Something had stopped the busy pens. The intimation that he only intended spending a few months in Ireland can have done little to improve relations. As it happened, he only stayed in Ireland about ten weeks.

He left London on the 31st May, and that night, from his first stopping place, he wrote to Vanessa,

I promised to write to you; and I have to let you know that it is impossible for anyone to have more acknowledgements at heart, for all your kindness & generosity to me. I hope this journey will restore my health: I will ride but little every day, and I will write a common letter to you all from some of my stages, but directed to you . . . Pray be merry, and eat and walk and be good and send me your commands . . . . I have hardly time to put pen to paper, but I would make good my promise. Pray God preserve you and make you happy and easy—and so adieu, brat.

Swift's last letter to the Ladies had been written more than a fortnight earlier; nor did they hear from him again until a week later, when the *Journal* ends, on the 6th June, at Chester.

He arrived in Dublin, some days later, to find himself in a hostile Whig community. On the day of his installation, a scurrilous verse was nailed to the door of his Cathedral. It was an open secret that it was the work of the Dean of Killala.

To-day, this Temple gets a Dean,*
Of parts and fame uncommon;

---

*As the "poet" was a bitter enemy of Swift, rumours of whose Temple paternity were already in circulation, this description of the church may not have been accidental!

Used both to pray, and to profane,
To serve both God & Mammon . . . .
This Place he got by wit and rhyme,
And many ways most odd;
And might a Bishop be in time,
Did he believe in God . . . .
Look down, St. Patrick, look, we pray
On thine own Church and Steeple;
Convert thy Dean on this great Day,
Or else, God help the People.

Swift was installed in his Deanery — the bitter-tanged fruit of his long political labours—and fled from Dublin to his country parish. In a letter to Vanessa from Laracor, dated the 8th July 1713, he describes his misery:

I stayed but a fortnight in Dublin, very sick; and returned not one visit of a hundred that were made me, but all to the Dean, and none to the Doctor. I am riding here for life, and think I am something better, and hate the thoughts of Dublin, and prefer a field-bed and an earthen floor before the great house there, which they say is mine. I had your last spleenatic letter. I told you when I left England I would endeavour to forget everything there and would write as seldom as I could . . . . I design to pass the greatest part of the time I stay in Ireland here in the cabin where I am now writing, neither will I leave the Kingdom till I am sent for; and if they have no further service for me I will never see England again. At my first coming I thought I should have died with discontent, and was horribly melancholy while they were installing me: but it began to wear off and change to dullness . . . . I must go to take my bitter draught to cure my head, which is really spoilt by the bitter draughts the public hath given me . . . . .

His black cloud of misery does not appear to have been much lightened by MD's presence. His accounts show that he spent less than twelve shillings on meals with them.

Swift had arranged to return to London before the winter, and Vanessa was, naturally, aware of the fact, but not prepared to be forgotten in the interval. In spite of his apparent prohibition, she had written four times before he replied from Laracor. Their mutual good friend, Erasmus Lewis, provided the cover. One of these letters ends:

> *I am impatient to the last degree to hear how you are. I hope I shall soon have you here.*

The next:

> *Pray let me hear from you soon, which will be an inexpressible joy to her that is always—*

Presumably in accordance with Swift's desire for caution, Vanessa signed none of her letters. He can have needed no signature to recognise the possessive love of the girl, who so confidently was counting the days till his return. She had not long to wait. At the end of August, Dean Swift left Ireland, and early in September was back in the whirling activities of London. The warmth of his welcome, both private and public, must have been singularly comforting after the bleak and hostile weeks in Ireland.

V

PROVERBIALLY, distance makes hearts grow fonder, and much wisdom is crystallised in these old sayings. It requires no vivid imagination to picture Vanessa's welcome. To Mrs. Van Homrigh the Dean was her daughter's accepted suitor, even if, for his own good reasons, the engagement still had to be kept secret. In spite of the new powers conferred by the Act of Parliament, little progress had been made in straightening out the Van Homrigh financial muddle; and there was no immediate prospect of Vanessa's dowry becoming available, in spite of the girl's distracted struggles with Mr. Partinton. Mrs. Van Homrigh would thoroughly sympathise with Swift's refusal to regard the Deanery of St. Patrick's as anything but a stepping-stone to his real aim: an appointment in England, worthy of his powers. Mrs. Van Homrigh had removed herself and her family from the Kingdom of Ireland; as stated in the *Petition*, they were *now residing and intended to make their residence in England.* She would have thoroughly agreed with the letter Swift wrote, before going to Dublin to take over his Deanery:

> *I am condemned to live again in Ireland, and all the Court and Ministry did for me was to let me choose my station in the country where I am banished.*

Nor were Swift's hopes of an English appointment over-sanguine. After all, the Bishop of Bristol had been made Lord Privy Seal, and Swift's good friend, Prior, had been appointed a Plenipotentiary to negotiate the Peace of Utrecht. A similar diplomatic appointment might well advance Swift's reputation so far that his claims to higher clerical honours could scarcely be refused, even by *the royal*

Prude — as Swift had described the Queen, somewhat unwisely, in a recent publication.

It is clear that the Dean returned to London with renewed zest for power and privilege, and that he soon established himself in higher favour than ever with the Tory Lords. By the end of 1713, he was again their chief adviser and pamphleteer.

No letters exist between Swift and Vanessa during those nine months—presumably, there was no need for them. Of their relationship, nothing can be said with certainty. The only clue to the situation is in the Burial Register of St. James's Church. Piccadilly.

10*th February* 1713-14, *Hester Van Homry.*

In her will, which has also been overlooked, Mrs. Van Homrigh states that she is *sick and weak in body, but (praise be to God for it) of sound and disposing mind and memory.* The will is dated the 16th January, 1713-14, and was put into probate on the 11th February following. She appointed her daughter, Esther, sole executrix, and left her, amongst other items, her diamond necklace and earrings, her wedding-ring, a ruby and diamond ring, as well as her *fur-tippett.* To her daughter, Mary, she bequeathed her pearl necklace and earrings, her cornelian and diamond ring and other valuables. Mrs. Van Homrigh also exercised the right she was given in her husband's will to leave £500 as she wished. She divided this sum, equally, between her three children on condition that her debts be paid. She also left her son, Bartholomew, *my silver dressing-plate, gold seal and large silver medal.*

From her statement that she was *sick and weak in body* in January, it seems probable that she may have been ill for some time. (So many of her family died young that it is possible they all had tuberculosis: her husband died in

1703-4, presumably still a young man; Ginkell died in 1710, aged about sixteen; Mary, after years of illness, died in 1720, aged about twenty-four and Bartholomew died in 1715, aged about twenty-two.)

Curiously enough, Dean Swift, in his letters to Ireland, appears to have made no reference whatever to the death of this lady, well known in Dublin society. In her will, she asks to be buried *in a decent but very private manner;* it is not known whether discretion prevented Dean Swift's attendance on the 10th February, at St. James's Church, when the kindly Mrs. Van Homrigh was buried near her wayward boy, Ginkell. Seven years later, when Mary Van Homrigh died after a long illness in Ireland he wrote to the distracted Vanessa:

> . . . . *For God's sake get your friends about you, to advise and to order everything in the forms. It is all you have to do. I want comfort myself in this case and can give little. Time alone must give it to you. Nothing is now your part but decency* . . . .

It is to be hoped that on the death of Mrs. Van Homrigh, Swift did not leave her daughters entirely to the good offices of their friends.

Swift was now at the pinnacle of his political career, cherished and flattered by the Tories and correspondingly loathed and feared by the Whigs. His recommendation was sufficient to job-seekers, high and low; but he was curiously ineffective for himself. He had been promised £1,000 to pay his out-of-pocket expenses in connection with his installation as Dean of St. Patrick's, and he had asked for the appointment of Historiographer. He got neither, to his justifiable indignation.

The intrigues around the obviously dying Queen became more and more frantic. The Whigs, their eyes firmly fixed on Hanover, were arrogantly sure of an early victory and openly vowing vengeance on their enemies, amongst whom Swift stood prominently. The times were dangerous, and he recognised that he could no longer hope to control the suicidal progress of the Tory Ministry. By the end of May, against the advice and pleadings of his friends, Swift left London for a quiet Berkshire village, there to await events.

VI

My informant was Richard Brennan, he is at present a bellringer in St. Patrick's and in a state of penury. (Such should not be the case, the servant in whose arms Swift breathed his last, and who attended him during the six years immediately preceding his death.) My informer, who is still living in Dublin, told me that when he was at school there was a boy boarded with the Master who was commonly reported to be the Dean's son by Mrs. Johnson. He added that the boy strongly resembled the Dean in his complexion, that he dined constantly at the Deanery on Sunday, and that when the other boys were driven out of the deanery yard, he was suffered to remain there and divert himself. This boy survived Mrs. Johnson by a year or two at most.

Monck Berkeley's *Literary Relics* Jan. 1789.

I received your letter when some company was with me on Saturday night; and it put me in such confusion that I could not tell what to do. I here send you the paper you left me. This morning a woman, who does business for me, told me she heard I was in love with one—naming you, and twenty particulars, that little master and I visited you, and that the A-B did so; and that you had an abundance of wit, etc. I ever feared the tattle of this nasty town and told you so; and that was the reason why I said to you long ago that I would see you seldom when you were in Ireland. And I must beg you to be easy if, for some time, I visit you seldomer, and not in so particular a manner. I will see you at the latter end of the week—if possible. These are accidents in life that are necessary and must be submitted to; and tattle, by the help of discretion, will wear off.

Swift to Vanessa, undated

I bequeath to Bryan M'Loghlin (a child who now lives with me and whom I keep on charity) twenty five pounds, to bind him an apprentice, as my executors and the survivors of them shall think fit.

Extract from the Will of Esther Johnson. 1727

SINCE the letters, which over years passed between Swift and Vanessa, provide the bulk of the evidence available for any assessment of their relationship, a short account of the subsequent history of this correspondence may be useful here.

In June 1723, Vanessa on her deathbed is believed to have given instructions for the publication of the letters and other papers, to one of her heirs, Robert Marshall, a young law-student. As she was an indefatigible letter-writer, it is extremely probable that she would have put such important instructions in writing, and it is very significant that no such document ever appeared in public, so that it is impossible to know whether her last wish was to embarrass and injure the man whom she had loved so deeply for sixteen years, or whether she believed the publication of her papers necessary to clear her memory of some grave imputation. The absence of any written instructions from Vanessa, together with the obvious removal of many of her carefully numbered letters, gives ample reason to believe that her papers were rigorously censored.

Her heirs and executors were the famous Dr. Berkeley—who could not remember ever having met her—and young Marshall, who may have been some distant connection.

Pleasantly surprised and grateful for their large and totally unexpected legacies, they arranged for the publication. According to Sheridan, writing in 1784, the manuscripts were *put to the press, and some progress made in the letters, when Dr. Sheridan getting intelligence of it . . . . . applied so effectively to the executors that the printed copy was cancelled, but the originals still remained in their hands.* One curious feature is that Dr. Berkeley (who was friendly to Swift) several times assured the Dean's very close friend Dr. Delany that the manuscripts contained *nothing which would either do honour to her character, or bring the least reflections upon Cadenus.* Either Dr. Berkeley had already carelessly edited the papers, suppressing anything he thought damaging to Swift, or else he had left the matter to young Mr. Marshall, who, not being so friendly to the Dean, was less careful about what went to the printer. It is certainly difficult to understand Dr. Berkeley's assurances.

There is, unfortunately, no way of knowing whether the material then given to the printer for publication is the same as the letters which subsequently made a first, partial appearance in 1767, forty-four years later. In that year, in an edition of Swift's letters printed for James Williams, Skinner's Row, Dublin, the following appears,

> *In the Appendix will be found some letters between the Dean and Mrs. Esther Vanhomrigh . . . . which did not come into the hands of the proprietors till the rest of the work was printed.*

It adds,

> *The originals of these letters are in the hands of a gentleman of great eminence in the Law in Ireland,*

A further note explains that the gentleman in question is:

> *Robert Marshall, Esq. late one of the Judges of His Majesty's Court of Common Pleas.*

Robert Marshall had been forced to retire from the Bench, by ill-health, some years previously, and was, in 1767, living in Co. Dublin, presumably still in possession of the Swift-Vanessa correspondence, which had been so long suppressed. Dean Swift and Marshall's co-executor, Bishop Berkeley, both being dead for many years, the retired Judge must have felt that he could at last do tardy justice to his benefactress, but whether the selection of letters published in 1767 was the same as that approved by Dr. Berkeley as not casting *the least reflection on Cadenus*, there is no way of knowing. Since Dr. Berkeley undoubtedly knew sufficient French to understand *Soyez assurée que jamais personne du monde a étè aimée, honorée, estimée, adorée par votre ami que vous*, one can only conclude that Dr. Berkeley saw nothing unfitting in an elderly Dean assuring a young woman of his adoration, so long as he did so in a foreign language.

What had become of the originals of the letters was a mystery until May 1919, when the Morrison collection was offered for sale at Sotheby's. It included a volume, bound in a fine calf cover, which contained what is described on its first page in an eighteenth century script as:

Original Letters of Dr. Jonathan Swift, Dean of St. Patrick's, Dublin to Mrs. Van Homrigh, celebrated by him in his published works under the name Vanessa.

With the foul copies of her Letters and Answers in her own Writing!

This volume was bought for the British Museum.

Various suggested explanations — including blackmail — have been offered for the fact that Vanessa made and preserved rough drafts of her letters to Swift. A simple reason for the *foul copies* could be that she was extremely conscious of the literary eminence of her correspondent and anxious to write as good a letter as she could. Since eighteenth century posts were very slow and erratic, a copy of her own last letter must have been almost essential in order to understand the deliberately enigmatic replies of Swift. The Dean himself both made and kept drafts of his letters to friends. This habit was probably widespread in an age when the art of letter-writing was both highly cultivated and much appreciated.

As to the charge of preserving Swift's letters, it is one which could be levelled against most lovers, since love became literate.

These letters, then, are all that now remains of the Correspondence between Cadenus, as Swift disguised himself, and Vanessa, and are worthy of some study.

Shortly after her death, one item amongst the papers did, somewhat mysteriously, find its way to the public: *Cadenus and Vanessa*, a long poem which Swift had written about ten years earlier. In this, he purports to give a history of their early relations. Its circulation, so soon after the flare of scandal following Vanessa's death, added a fierce fuel to the fire. Some idea of the atmosphere in Dublin can be given by a letter, written by Dr. Evans, Bishop of Meath, to the Archbishop of Canterbury, within a few weeks of Vanessa's death.

> *I think it not improper for me to acquaint your Grace with a passage lately happened here wherein Jonathan Swift is said to be pretty much concerned. A young woman, Mrs. Van Omrig (a pretended vain wit), and ye Dean had great friendship, many letters & papers passed betwixt them (the subject I know nothing of); they give out, there was a marriage promise between them, but this I can't affirm ... In April, last, she discovered the D was married to Mrs. Johnson (a natural daughter of Sir W. Temple, a very good woman), upon which she expressed great indignation, making a new will and leaving all to Dr. Berkeley of this College . . . and to one Mr. Marshall, who was charged by her (on her deathbed) to print all the letters and papers*

which had passed between the D and herself . . . Ye Archbishop of Dublin and ye whole Irish posse have (I fear) prevailed with Mr. Marshall (ye lady's executor) not to print the papers, etc., as she desired, lest one of their own dear joyes should be trampled on by the Philistines.

The whole Irish posse may indeed have been working, as the Bishop complains, to protect the reputation of *one of their own dear joyes,* but the Dean himself had long fled the battlefield. Obviously fearing some shattering scandal, on the news of Vanessa's death, he immediately left Dublin, without leaving any address, even to his Cathedral clergy. Stella and her companion had already taken refuge in the country, after Swift's mysterious break with Vanessa. None of them returned to Dublin for many months.

It would be very interesting to know who spread the story that there had been *a promise of marriage* between the dead woman and the Dean, and what foundation existed for the statement. It is at least possible that amongst the papers Vanessa directed Mr. Marshall to publish was a copy of the Van Homrigh *Family Petition.* As her mother's executrix, she would certainly have had one.

The Bishop of Meath—enemy though he was to Swift—would not have dared to write such a complaint to the Archbishop of Canterbury, unless he were quite certain that there was a well-established fire to account for such volumes of acrid smoke.

VII

TO revert to 1714: some four months after Vanessa's mother's death Swift left London for Berkshire, spending a few days in Oxford. When he writes to Vanessa on 8th June 1714, he is in lodgings as he explains, with the Rev. Mr. Geree, who held an Oxford College living at Letcombe Bassett, a couple of miles from Wantage in Berkshire.

He addresses the letter to—

Mrs. Esther Van-homrigh
at her lodgings over against the Surgeon's, in Great Rider Street near St. James's Street,
London.

This address was almost certainly incorrect, as his three subsequent letters are addressed to,

Mrs. Van-Homrigh, at Mr.
Handcock's house in Little Ryder
Street, near St. James's Street
London.

It would seem that Vanessa and her sister had moved to new lodgings immediately after Swift's departure from London, and that he did not remember the correct address. This is important when considering the post-script of this letter which Vanessa has numbered I:

You see I am better than my word, and write to you before I have been a week settled in the house where I am. I have not much news to tell you from hence, nor have I one line from anybody since I left London, of which I am very glad. But to say the truth, I believe I shall not stay here so long as I intended. I am at a clergyman's house, an old friend and acquaintance, whom I love very well; but he is such a melancholy thoughtful man, partly from nature and partly by a solitary life, that I shall soon catch the spleen from him . . . . His wife has been this month twenty miles off at her father's and will not return this ten days. I never saw her, and perhaps the house will be worse when she comes. I read all day, or walk, and do not speak as many words as I have now writ, in three days. So that in short, I have a mind to steal away to Ireland, unless I find myself take more to this way of living, so different in every circumstance from what I have left. This is the first syllable I have writ to anyone since you saw me. I shall be glad to hear from you, not as you are a Londoner, but a friend. For I care not threepence for news, nor have heard one syllable since I am here. The Pretender or the Duke of Cambridge may both be landed, and I never the wiser. But if this place were ten times worse, nothing shall make me return to Town while things are in the situation I left them . . . . I hope you are in good health and humour. My service to Moll. My cold is quite gone.

A vous etc.

I send my man two miles with this to the post town, so if there is a letter by chance from you, I shall not be able to tell you so now. I hope our maid carried your bandbox with the papers and deeds.

Unfortunately, Vanessa's reply is missing, as the next letter is numbered 3.

Several things in Swift's letter are worth noting. Apparently he suggests to Vanessa, for the first time, that he may possibly go over to Ireland, instead of remaining in Berkshire as he had intended. He also stresses the change in his manner of life, *so different in every circumstance from what I left.* And he ends with the surprising query whether *our maid carried your bandbox with the papers and deeds?*—

presumably as part of Vanessa's move to new lodgings, from some other where they had shared a maid.

The use of the word *friend* may be noted; but apart from Swift's constant caution and fear of letters being intercepted, he often used the word where a much more affectionate relationship is obvious. (In a later letter to Vanessa, who was a most devoted sister to Moll, Swift hopes *to see the sincerest friendship in the world long between you.*)

Some of the inexplicable happenings in the future might be explained by the assumption that Swift and this young woman who had never made any secret of her passionate love had been living together since his return to London in the Autumn of 1713. She considered herself his affianced wife; his most ardent defenders have never suggested that he was impervious to female charms. Swift had himself painted a glowing picture of sexual delights to an earlier love, *Varina*, (Miss Waring, daughter of the Archdeacon of Dromore, Co. Antrim.)

> *Surely, Varina, you have but a mean opinion of the joys that accompany a true, honourable unlimited love; yet either nature and our ancestors have hugely deceived us, or else all sublunary things are dross in comparison. Is it possible you cannot be yet unsensible to the prospect of a rapture and delight so innocent and so exalted? Trust me, Varina, Heaven has given us nothing else worth the loss of a thought. Ambition, high appearance, friends and fortune are all tasteless and insipid when they come in competition; yet millions of such glorious minutes we are perpetually losing, for ever losing, irrecoverably losing, to gratify empty forms and wrong notions . . . . To resist the violence of our inclinations in the beginning is a strain of self denial that may have some pretences to set up for a virtue; but when they are grounded at first upon reason, when they have taken firm root and grown to a height, it*

is folly—folly as well as injustice—to withstand their dictates; for this passion has a property peculiar to itself, to be more commendable in its extremes; and it is as possible to err in the excess of piety as of love.

To young, adoring Vanessa, the expression of such sentiments would be preaching to the converted. For several years, she had considered herself Swift's wife in all but name. She was alone in the world except for a delicate young sister and an unsatisfactory absent brother. She was her own mistress.

Some of Swift's most intimate friends were notorious, even by Eighteenth Century standards, for their lax morals—royal mistresses or ex-mistresses always ranked high in his esteem. He certainly was no prude. Under the conditions, he would have had to be superhuman to resist the loving young woman, whom he obviously found extremely attractive.

The letter to Varina quoted above, includes one sentence which might well serve as an epitaph to the story of Swift and Vanessa,

Love, with the gall of too much Discretion, is a thousand times worse than with none at all.

This *discretion* which Swift both practised himself and exacted from others, hangs like a fog over all their lives, only lifting occasionally to allow a tantalising glimpse of the truth. But the Dean must himself eventually have realised the havoc it could produce, for a poem was found, in his handwriting, amongst Vanessa's papers after her death. It ends—

. . . . curst Discretion, all the fault was thine;
Cupid and Hymen thou hast set at odds
And bred such feuds between those kindred gods
That Venus cannot reconcile her sons;

When one appears, away the other runs.
The former scales, wherein he used to poise
Love against love, and equal joys and joys
Are now filled up with avarice and pride,
Where titles, power and riches still subside.
Thou, gentle Venus, to thy father run
And tell him how thy children are undone;
Prepare his bolts to give one fatal blow
And send Discretion to the shades below!

In June 1714, Swift would have considered discretion more essential than ever, if Vanessa were about to have a child — that unexplained boy, who intrudes at least four times into Swift's later life.

Two letters are missing from the Correspondence, after his first letter from Letcombe. The next, a month later, numbered 3 by Vanessa, is almost entirely dealing with business arising from Mrs. Van Homrigh's death, and with his offers to be security, should Vanessa need to borrow money from his printers. The next letter, numbered 5, refers to two letters she had written, but which are also missing from the Correspondence. In this letter Swift tells her that he had actually made arrangements to go to Ireland, but had postponed his departure in order to visit Lord Oxford, who had finally been dismissed by the Queen, leaving Lord Bolingbroke to lead the Tory Ministry. Swift tells Vanessa that:

I expect to leave this in two or three days, one way or another . . . I am not of your opinion about Lord Bolingbroke. Perhaps he may get the Staff, but I cannot rely on his love for me. He knew I had a mind to be Historiographer, though I value it not but for the public service; yet it is gone to a worthless rogue that nobody knows. I am writ to earnestly by somebody to come to Town and join these people in power, but I will not do it.

The worthless rogue that nobody knows was the eminent historian, Thomas Madox, author of *The History and Antiquities of the Exchequer of the Kings of England*, published some years previously. Swift was not always fair to his opponents.

The letter ends with instructions for the repair of some of his knives, which he has left in her keeping, giving her the address of *my toy-man in Exchange Alley*. And he adds,

> *Where's your discretion in desiring to travel with that body?*

that body being Swift's printer and close associate, Barber, who visited him in Letcombe, and with whom Vanessa had, possibly, suggested she might visit Swift there.

Although he was unaware of it, Queen Anne was already dead when Swift wrote this letter. On the first day of August 1714 the Stuart dynasty had lost their last tenuous grip on the throne and the Hanoverians had, curiously, become the British Royal Family. Vanessa's hopes that Lord Bolingbroke would re-establish Swift's fortunes had vanished with the Queen's last breath.

The realisation that he had actually considered leaving for Ireland without seeing her again was obviously too much for Vanessa. Swift's next letter to her, dated twelve days later, reproaches her—again—for her want of discretion.

> *I had your letter last post, and before you can send me another I shall set out for Ireland. I must go and take the oaths, and the sooner the better. I think, since I have known you, I have drawn an old house upon my head. You used to brag you were very discreet. Where is it gone? It is probable I may not stay in Ireland long, but be back by the beginning of winter. When I am there, I will write to you as soon as I can conveniently, but it shall always be under cover; and if you write to me, let some other direct*

it; and I beg you will write nothing that is particular, but which may be seen; for I apprehend letters will be opened and inconvenience happen. If you are in Ireland while I am there, I shall see you very seldom. It is not a place for any freedom; but is is probable we may meet in London in winter, or if not, leave all to Fate, that seldom cares to humour our inclinations. I say all this out of the perfect esteem and friendship I have for you. These public misfortunes have altered all my measures and broke my spirits. God almighty bless you. I shall, I hope, be on horseback in a day after this comes to your hand. I would not answer your questions for a million, nor can I think of them with any ease of mind. Adieu.

This letter, addressed to her *at Mr. Handcock's in Little Rider Street*—Mr. Handcock being, presumably, *the Surgeon* of the address of the first letter Swift wrote after they parted in London—refers to yet another indiscretion; the visit she had paid him a very short time previously. It is not clear, from his reproaches, whether the very idea of the visit had alarmed him, or whether he merely objected to the fact that Vanessa had travelled to Letcombe through so public a place as the Post-town, Wantage. But in later times, *the Berkshire Surprise* took its place in the litany of happy memories of which he used to remind her. He explains to her that he now *must* go to Dublin to take the oath of loyalty to the new King, as Dean of S. Patrick's; and that he hopes to be back again in England by the Winter. If he knew that there was no question of her being able to travel to Ireland for some months, then he may well have hoped that the prospect of his speedy return would keep her safely in London. Since Vanessa's difficulties in getting control of her estate could be more easily solved in Mr. Partinton's Dublin office than in London, she had every excuse to make a visit to Ireland, and must have discussed such a visit with Swift.

So it is significant to read his warning that, if she *should* decide to come to Ireland, it would be practically impossible for them to meet there. His almost hysterical accounts of the dangers of being seen together in Dublin sound a note which was still echoing and re-echoing many years later, and raise the immediate queries: *what* was he so anxious to hide, and *what* were the questions this girl had asked him, which he would not answer *for a million,* the very thought of which robbed his mind of all its ease? Whatever the answers may be, Swift left his retreat in Berkshire, and travelled to Dublin in the middle of August 1714; and Vanessa, whose every instinct must have urged her to follow, remained behind in the Surgeon's house, Little Rider St., for almost three months.

VIII

A FEW weeks after Swift's return to Dublin, he wrote some verses which give a vivid picture of his state of mind.

In sickness.

'Tis true . . . then why should I repine
To see my life so fast decline?
But, why obscurely and alone,
Where I am neither loved nor known?
My state of health none care to learn;
My life is here no soul's concern:
And those with whom I now converse,
Without a tear will tend my hearse.
Some formal visits, looks and words,
What mere humanity affords
I meet perhaps from three or four,
From whom I once expected more;
Which those who tend the sick for pay
Can act as decently as they;
But no obliging tender friend
To help at my approaching end,
My life is now a burthen grown
To others, e'er it be my own.

Even allowing for his illness and subsequent depression, it seems quite clear that Stella was not at hand, in her old capacity of devoted confidant and attendant, and that she is numbered amongst those from whom he *once expected more*. Presumably, too many stories of the *obliging, tender friend* in London had reached her ears, in Dublin. Nevertheless, in spite of his desire for the warm devotion of Vanessa, he must have heard of her impending arrival with dismay. But, since the advantages of dealing with her complicated law-affairs on the spot were so indisputable, it was impossible to dissuade her. Apart from the joy of being near him again, Vanessa must have been extremely conscious of the urgent importance of freeing her fortune from Mr. Partinton's clutches. She was well aware that it was an essential condition for their marriage, just as a suitable English appointment for the Dean was another.

And so, somewhere during the early days of November, 1714, Vanessa set out on what she believed would be a short visit to Dublin. She was accompanied on the long, wearisome journey by her delicate young sister, Moll, and her servants. Possibly not by Ann Kindon, who had been servant to Mrs. Van Homrigh in London. Many years later, she and her daughter figured as beneficiaries in Vanessa's Will, after many years' faithful service. Ann Kindon may have been left behind in London in charge of an infant.

To Mrs. Van-homrigh
at her lodgings in Turn-Stile Alley,
near College Green, Dublin.

Philipstown,
November 5th, 1714

I met your servant when I was a mile from Trim and could send him no other answer than I did, for I was going abroad by appointment. Besides I would not have gone to Kildrohid [Celbridge] *to see you for all the world: I ever told you that you wanted discretion. I am going to a friend upon a promise, and shall stay with him about a fortnight, and then come to Town; and I will call upon you as soon as I can, supposing you lodge in Turnstile Alley, as your servant told me, and that your neighbours can tell me your whereabouts. Your servant said you would be in Town on Monday; so I suppose this will be ready to welcome you there. I fear you had a journey full of fatigues: pray take care of your health in this Irish air, to which you are a stranger. Does not Dublin look very dirty to you, and the country miserable? Is Kildrohid as beautiful as Windsor, and as agreeable to you as the Prebend's Lodgings there? Is there any walk about you as pleasant as Marlborough Lodge? I have rode a tedious journey to-day, and can say no more. Nor shall you know where I am till I come, and then I will see you. A fig for your letters and messages. Adieu.*

This letter Vanessa has numbered I, as if she were opening a new series with her arrival in Ireland. Her letters to which Swift refers have not survived. All that is therefore certain is that Vanessa had recently arrived in Ireland, presumably with her delicate young sister, and had gone to the fine mansion, outside Celbridge, which her father had built.

This house is usually referred to as Marley Abbey, although it did not bear that name for years after Vanessa's death, when the Marley family bought the estate. It is ten miles from Dublin, and the river Liffey flows through its handsome pleasure grounds. Turnstile Alley, where the Van Homrighs had their town house, was a fashionable quarter in the Eighteenth Century, situated as it was off College Green, beside Chichester House where the Parliament met. It was a short distance from Dublin Castle and from Trinity College. It was also close to the Deanery of St. Patrick's. The house in Turnstile Alley had almost certainly been her father's house; as a Member of Parliament, he would have found it very convenient. It was also the house which Archbishop King advised Vanessa to sell, some years later, when her financial difficulties became acute. It is important to remember that Vanessa had a town and country house, and that she moved frequently between them.

Apparently, her first stay in Celbridge was short; Swift having made it perfectly clear that, under no circumstances would he visit her there. It is of interest to note that he never *did* visit her in Celbridge until August, 1720—almost six years after her arrival in Ireland.

Swift's letter, stressing as it does the inferiority of the Irish scene to that she had just left behind her in London, was obviously intended to discourage her from any lengthy stay. It certainly sounded no note of welcome and must have given little comfort to Vanessa, after her *journey full of fatigues*.

The next letter, undated and endorsed *3rd*, is addressed to *Misshess Vanr* and is, presumably, a hand-delivered note.

> *I will see you to-morrow, if possible. You know it is not above five days since I saw you and that I would ten times more if it were at all convenient, whether your old dragon came or no, whom I believe my people cannot tell what to make of, but take him for some conjurer.*
>
> *Adieu, Tuesday morning, ten*

The old dragon who looked so strange to the Deanery staff, was probably a liveried man-servant whom she had brought with her from London. All that can be gathered, from Swift's somewhat enigmatic note is that Swift had been visiting her fairly frequently in her Dublin house and that he protests that he would have done so very much more often had it been *convenient*—which may be translated *discreet*—to do so.

The next letter, endorsed *4th*, is merely dated *Dublin*, 1714, and was also, almost certainly, delivered by hand. It is, like all the other correspondence, unsigned, and is to Swift from Vanessa. In this letter, she appears for the first time as the highly temperamental, emotional young woman, whom Swift later used to refer to as *Governor Huff* and beg not to quarrel with him. She was a victim of that

Eighteenth Century epidemic, *the Spleen*, and the correspondence is full of allusions to her feeling *so low*. In a later letter the Dean complains, *I am confident you came chiding into the world, and will continue so while you are in it.* While admitting that Vanessa was a neurotic young woman, it is also clear that this attractive, intelligent, capable girl was extremely unfortunate in the situation in which she found herself, and that under happier conditions she would have been an unfrustrated, contented and devoted wife.

You cannot but be sensible, at least in some degree, of the many uneasinesses I am slave to — a wretch of a brother, cunning executors and importunate creditors of my mother's — things I can in no way avoid being subject to at present, and weighty enough to sink greater spirits than mine without some support. Once I had a friend that would see me sometimes, and either commend what I did or advise me what to do, which banished all my uneasiness. But now, when my misfortunes are increased by being in a disagreeable place, amongst strange, prying, deceitful people, whose company is so far from an amusement that it is a very great punishment you fly from me and give me no reason but that we are amongst fools and must submit. I am very well satisfied that we are amongst such but know no reason for having my happiness sacrificed to their caprice. You once had a maxim, which was to act what was right and not mind what the world said. I wish you would keep it now. Pray what can be wrong in seeing and advising an unhappy young woman? I can't imagine. You can't but know that your frowns make my life unsupportable. You have taught me to distinguish, and then you leave me miserable. Now all I beg is that you will for once counterfeit (since you can't otherwise) that indulgent friend you once were, till I get the better of these difficulties, for my sister's sake; for were not she involved (who, I know, is not so able to manage them as I am), I have a nobler soul than to sit struggling with misfortunes, when at the end I can't promise myself any real happiness. Forgive me; and I beg you'd believe it is not in my power to avoid complaining as I do.

The tone of the letter is very interesting; although she asks, or rather demands his help, she does so as one who has a perfect right to do so, clearly implying that his discretion in dealing with her affairs is mere weakness and subservience to public gossips — the *strange, prying, deceitful people* to whom she refers. Turnstile Alley being a short distance from Capel Street, where the Ladies then lodged, it is easy to imagine the buzzing of rumour. Her *wretch of a brother*, Bartholomew, owed a considerable amount to his mother's estate, which was still unpaid in May, 1715, when his Will was proved.

As usual when Vanessa really gets carried away, Swift abjectly surrenders, whether from genuine love of the girl, or from fear of what she might do, if driven too far. His letter is undated, addressed to *Miss Hessy Van* and presumably delivered by hand.

I will see you in a day or two, and believe me, it goes to my soul not to see you oftener. I will give you the best advice countenance and assistance I can. I would have been with you sooner if a thousand impediments had not prevented me. I did not imagine you had been under difficulties. I am sure my whole fortune should go to remove them. I cannot see you, I fear, to-day, having affairs of my place to do; but pray think it not want of friendship or tenderness, which I will always continue to the utmost. *Monday morning.*

Some short time later, Vanessa writes another letter, dated 1714. From it, it is obvious that the girl has had a very serious quarrel with Swift, in the course of which his terrible anger — so much feared by his closest associates — has had its way. As this is, it seems, the last existing letter for a considerable time, the fateful year 1714 ends with this explosion of Vanessa's misery.

Well, now I see plainly how great a regard you have for me. You bid me be easy, and you'd see me as often as you could. You had better said, as often as you could get the better of your inclinations so much, or as often as you remembered there was such a one in the world. If you continue to treat me as you do you will not be made uneasy by me long. 'Tis impossible to describe what I have suffered since I saw you last; those killing, killing words of yours. Sometimes I have resolved to die without seeing you more; but those resolves, to your misfortune, did not last long. For there is something in human nature that prompts one so to find relief in this world, I must give way to it, and beg you'd see me and speak kindly to me; for I am sure you'd not condemn anyone to suffer what I have done, could you but know it. The reason I write to you is because I cannot tell it to you, should I see you; for when I begin to complain, you are angry, and there is something in your look so awful, that it strikes me dumb. Oh! that you may but have so much regard for me left, that this complaint may touch your soul with pity. I say as little as ever I can: did you but know what I thought, I am sure it would move you. Forgive me, and believe I cannot help telling you this, and live.

After that letter, there is silence, until a note from Swift, which may well be dated 1715 because of the allusion to Dr. Pratt, Provost of Trinity College, who was an executor of the will of Vanessa's brother, Bartholomew. At his recent death, May 1715, he left his estate for life, to his sisters, so it seems natural that Vanessa should be in touch with Dr. Pratt.

(In Bartholomew Van Homrigh's will, which was put into probate by Dr. Pratt and Peter Partington on the 15th May, 1715, he left directions for the immediate repayment of the money he owed to his mother's estate for the expenses of his very considerable travel, as well as for his board and lodging while living in her London household. This will was drawn up in London, within a few weeks of his mother's death. He left a legacy to *Mr. Thomas Bacon of the Middle Temple, London* — presumably the same Thomas Bacon who had recently witnessed his mother's will. He also left a legacy to the Rev. Mr. Periam, *heretofore my Tutor in Christchurch, Oxford.* and to Erasmus Lewis.

Although Bartholomew states that he is *in good health of body*, his will seems oddly pessimistic for a young man of twenty-two. He shows an almost frantic desire for the perpetuation of the name, Van Homrigh, either through his father's godson, Bartholomew Partington, should he consent to assume that name, or, failing such consent, by the erection of a Van Homrigh building in Trinity College, Dublin. At twenty-two, he apparently believed himself incapable of fathering a child.)

The note was obviously written by Swift in Vanessa's house in Turnstile Alley.

I dined with the Provost and told him I was coming here, because I must be at prayers at six. He said you had been with him, and would not be at home this day, and went to Celbridge tomorrow. I said I would however go try. I fancy you told him so that he might not come tonight. If he comes you must piece it up as you can, else he will think it was on purpose to meet me, and I hate anything that looks like a secret. I cannot possibly call after prayers, and therefore came here in the afternoon, while people were at Church, hoping certainly to find you. I am truly afflicted for poor Moll, who is a girl of infinite value; I am sure you will take all possible care of her; and I hope to live to see the sincerest friendship in the world long between you. I pray God of Heaven protect you both, and am entierement—

Four o'clock.

After that note there is nothing, until a very long letter, written by Swift, in French, dated 12th May, 1719. It is addressed to *Madame Hester Vanhumri*, and begins by explaining that it is not true that he has left Dublin for three months; that he has merely gone to visit some friends in the country to improve his health. He continues,

Croyez moy, s'il y a chose croyable au monde, que-je pense tout ce que vous pouvez souhaiter de moy, et que tous vos desirs seront toujours obèi comme des commandements qu'il sera impossible de violer.

After warm good wishes for her health and hopes that she will spend part of the summer in her Celbridge home, he continues,

Il faut vous connoitre long temps de connoitre toutes vos perfections; toujours en vous voyant et entendant il en paroissent des nouvelles, qui estoient auparavent cachées . . . vous, qui estes incapable d'aucune sottise, si ce n'est l'estime qu'il vous plaist d'avoir pour moy. Car il n'y a point de merite, ni aucun preuve de mon bon goût de trouver en vous tout ce que la Nature a donne a un mortel. Je veux dire l'honneur, la vertue, le bon sens l'esprit, la doueur, l'agrement et la fermité d'ame. Mais en vous cachant commes vous faites, le monde ne vous connoit pas, et vous perdez l'eloge des millions de gens.

Depuis que j'ai l'honneur de vous connoitre, j'ay toujours remarqué que ni en conversation particuliere ni generale aucun mot a echappe de votre bouche, qui pouvoit etre mieux exprimé; et je vous jure qu'en faisant souvent la plus severe critique, je ne pouvois jamais trouver aucun defaut, ni en vos actions ni en vos parolles. La coquetrie, l'affectation, la pruderie sont des imperfections que vous n'avez jamais connu. Et avec tout cela, croyez vous qu'il est possible de ne vous estimer au dessus du reste du genre humain? Quelle bestes en juppes sont les plus excellentes de celles que je vois semées dans le monde au prix de vous. En les voyant, en les entendant, je dis cent fois le jour, Ne parle, ne regarde, ne pense, ne fait rien comme ces miserables. Sont ce du meme sexe, du meme espece de creatures? Quel cruantè de faire mepriser autant de gens, qui sans songer de vous seront assès supportable. Mais il est tems de vous delasser, et dire adieu avec tous le respecte, la sincerete et l'estime du monde. Je suis et sera toujours — — — — —.

If, as Lord Orrery charged, Vanessa was *in her own opinion superior to all her sex,* she had Swift's authority for it. *What beasts in petticoats are the most excellent of those I see everywhere in comparison with you . . . What cruelty to make so many people appear despicable, who would seem tolerable if I didn't remember you.* And Swift ends this letter with five dashes, to be filled in by the loving heart of the girl to whom he had written this truly remarkable letter.

Obviously, the lovers had reached some *modus vivendi,* although, with Swift's temperament, it was not very stable.

There is a curious, undated letter, written to Vanessa, and obviously delivered to her Dublin house.

I received your letter when some company was with me on Saturday night; and it put me in such confusion, that I could not tell what to do. I here send you the paper you left me. This morning, a woman who does business for me, told me she heard I was in love with one—naming you, and twenty particulars, that little master and I visited you, and that the A-B did so; and that you had an abundance of wit, etc. I ever feared the tattle of this nasty town, and told you so; and that was the reason why I said to you, long ago, that I would see you seldom in Ireland. And I must beg you to be easy if for some time I visit you seldomer, and not in so particular a manner. I will see you at the latter end of the week if possible. These are accidents in life that are necessary and must be submitted to; and tattle by the help of discretion, will wear off. Monday morning, ten o'clock.

Discretion *had* indeed been lacking, if the conversation Swift reports were true. But, remembering that proud, violent-tempered man, whom even his best friends took very good care not to annoy; remembering Orrery's description of him *when the sternness of his visage was increased by rage, it is scarce possible to imagine looks, or features, that carried on them more terror;* remembering Vanessa's complaint that anger produced in him *looks so awful* as to strike her dumb, *is* it possible to believe the story? No woman, or man, from his Archbishop down, would have dared, or been permitted, to repeat such tittle-tattle to the Dean of St. Patrick's. To imagine that formidable man listening patiently, while some female caller repeated local gossip, *with twenty particulars*, is impossible. It is an incredible story.

Some other explanation must be found. It may well be that, finding his relationship had got out of control, Swift used the gossip of a fictitious woman to explain or excuse a general tightening up. But the accusations he repeats are extremely interesting. Apart from the charge of being in love with Vanessa—with *twenty particulars*—there is also the assertion *that little master and I visited you.* The question naturally arises, who was *little master*, whose visits to Vanessa were giving food for scandalous gossip?

If Vanessa had had a son, about October 1714—the child, whose imminent birth prevented her from following Swift to Ireland in the August of that year — he would now be about five or six years old. Once Vanessa had realised that there was little chance of Swift's speedy return to England, and that her own disastrous legal affairs would drag on indefinitely, she would have arranged to have their child in her neighbourhood. Visits of the boy to her house, arranged so as to coincide with Swift's, might well have seemed to Vanessa a way of strengthening their bond. To the Dean, such an arrangement would have appeared appallingly dangerous, but his position was so full of pitfalls that he could only act with extreme caution. Rather than refuse, openly, to continue such meetings—so running the risk of driving Vanessa to unknown lengths — he may have invented the story of the tattling woman, using it as a perfectly reasonable excuse for greater discretion. Vanessa herself would have had to acknowledge the danger to the Dean of such a discovery, and the disastrous results it would have on his career, both in and outside Ireland.

The fact that his letter ends with the promise of visiting her within a few days would seem to discount any genuine alarm on his part, about the *tattle of this nasty town.*

The next long letter from Vanessa is undated, but is assigned to about 1720. Although she complains, yet there is gaiety and confidence in her tone, and, apparently, her complaint is that he doesn't visit her every day.

Is it possible that again you will do the very same thing I warned you of so lately? I believe you thought I only rallied when I told you, the other night, I would pester you with letters. Did not I know you very well, I should think you knew but little of the world, to imagine that a woman would not keep her word whenever she promised anything that was malicious. Had not you better a thousand times throw away one hour, at some time or other of the day, than to be interrupted in your business at this rate? For I know 'tis as impossible for you to burn my letters without reading them, as 'tis for me to avoid reproving you when you behave yourself so wrong. Once more I advise you, if you have any regard for your quiet, to alter your behaviour quickly; for I do assure you I have too much spirit to sit contented with this treatment. Now, because I love frankness extremely, I here tell you that I have determined to try all manner of human arts to reclaim you, and if all those fail, I am resolved to have recourse to the black one, which it is said, never does. Now see what inconveniences you will bring both me and yourself into. Pray think calmly of it. Is it not much better to come of yourself than to be brought by force, and that, perhaps, at a time when you have the most agreeable engagement in the world? For when I undertake anything, I don't love to do it by halves. But there is one thing that falls out very luckily for you, which is that, of all the passions, revenge hurries me least, so that you have it yet in your power to turn all this fury into good humour, and, depend upon it, and more I assure you. Come at what time you please, you can never fail of being very well received.

To which Swift replied, with equally light-hearted banter,

If you write as you do, I shall come the seldomer, on purpose to be pleased with your letters, which I never look into without wondering how a Brat, who cannot read, can possibly write so well. You are mistaken; send me a letter without your hand on the outside, and I hold you a crown I shall not read it. But, raillery apart, I think it inconvenient for a hundred reasons that I should make your house a sort of constant dwellingplace. I will certainly come as often as I conveniently can, but my health and the perpetual run of ill weather hinders me from going out in the morning; and my afternoons are taken up, I know not how, that I am in rebellion with a dozen people beside yourself, for not seeing them. For the rest, you need make use of no other black art besides your ink. 'Tis a pity your eyes are not black, or I would have said the same of them; but you are a white witch and can do no mischief. If you have employed any of your art on the black scarf, I defy it, for one reason: guess. Adieu.

Eight years before, in London, she had made him another black scarf, which may provide the clue to Swift's invitation to *guess*.

In July, 1720, Swift wrote to her, to her house in Celbridge:

I am now writing on Wednesday night, when you are hardly settled at home; and it is the first hour of leisure I have had, and it may be Saturday before you have it, and then there will be Governor Huff; and to make you more so, I here enclose a letter to poor Malkin, which I will command her not to show you, because it is a love-letter. I reckon by this time the groves and fields and purling streams have made Vanessa romantic, provided poor Malkin be well. Your friend sent me the verses he promised, which I here transcribe:

Nymph, would you learn the only art
To keep a worthy lover's heart,
First, to adorn your person well
In utmost cleanliness excell;
And though you must the fashions take,
Observe them but for fashion's sake.

The strongest reason will submit
To virtue, honour, sense and wit.
To such a nymph, the wise and good
Cannot be faithless, if they would:
For vices all have different ends
But virtue still to virtue tends:
And when your lover is not true,
'Tis virtue fails, in him or you;
And either he deserves disdain,
Or you without a cause complain.
But here Vanessa cannot err,
Nor are these rules applied to her:
For who would such a nymph forsake
Except a blockhead or a rake?
Or how could she her heart bestow
Except where wit and virtue grow?

In my opinion these lines are too grave, and therefore may not fit you, who I fear are in the spleen; but that is not fit either for yourself or the person you tend, to whom you ought to read diverting things. Here is an epigram that concerns you not:

Dorinda dreams of dress a-bed,
'Tis all her thought and art;
Her lace hath got within her head
Her stays stick in her heart.

If you do not like these things, what must I say? This town yields no better. The questions which you were used to ask me, you may suppose to be all answered, just as they used to be after half an hour debate — entendez-vous cela? You are to have a number of parsons in your neighbourhood, but not one that you love, for your age of loving parsons is not yet arrived. What this letter wants in length it will have in difficulty, for I believe you cannot read it. I will write plainer to Malkin, because she is not much used to my hand. I hold a wager there are some lines in this letter you will not understand, though you can read them. So drink your coffee and remember you are a desperate chip, and that the lady who calls you bastard will be ready to answer all your questions. 'Tis now Sunday night before I could finish this.

Swift wrote this letter over five days, taking up the thread of easy thought as time offered, in affectionately jocose style. The mysterious *lady who calls you bastard* and who was ready to supply all answers is probably Venus. In the poem *Cadenus and Vanessa,* she assures her fellow-goddess that the infant Vanessa so closely resembles Cupid that she appears to be a child of Apollo. The answering of *questions,* which appears so often in the later letters, first poses its enigma here, and, because he is not certain that *she* will understand the phrase, he adds *Entendez-vous cela*?

In her reply from Celbridge, 28th July, 1720, she makes it clear that she does understand.

I thought I should have heard from you in a week, according to your promise, but that week consisted of fourteen days, which were to me, after the first seven, very long, long ones. I own I never expected to have another letter from you, for two reasons: first, because I thought you had quite forgot me, and because I was so very ill that I thought I should have died. But, ever since I received your letter, which was last Friday, I have been pretty well. I have done all that lay in my power to follow your example, for fear of teasing you, but I find I cannot defer writing to you any longer. When I opened your letter, I thought you had wrote me two, as you said perhaps you might; but instead of that to find 'twas a letter to another, and that a love-letter — how do you think I could support it? But upon my word, when I see you I have a vast deal to say to you about that letter. I have asked you all the questions I used, ten thousand times, and don't find them answered at all to my satisfaction.

The letters *poor Malkin* got from Swift have not survived, but the kindness which prompted his notes to the dying girl is one of his pleasanter traits. Mary Van Homrigh had apparently been in bad health since he had first known her. In July, 1720, she had only a few months to live. Almost certainly, in nursing her, Vanessa had herself become infected with tuberculosis; and the psychological stresses which that disease produces are added, from now on, to the other tensions which drove Vanessa to her early grave.

Swift to Vanessa:

If you knew how many little difficulties there are in sending letters to you, it would remove five parts or six of your quarrell; but since you lay hold of my promises, and are so exact to the day, I shall promise you no more, and rather choose to be better than my word, than worse. I am confident that you came chiding into the world, and will continue so while you are in it. I was in great apprehension that poor Malkin was worse, and till I could be satisfied on that particular, I would not write again. But I little expected to have heard of your own ill health, and those who saw you since made no mention to me of it. I wonder what Malkin meant by shewing you my letter: I will write to her no more, since she can keep secrets no better. It was the first love-letter I have writ these dozen years, and since I have so ill success I will write no more — never was a belle passion so defeated. But the Governor, I hear, is jealous and upon your word you have a vast deal to say to me about it. Mind your nurse-keeping, do your duty and leave off your huffing. One would think you were in love, by dating your letter August 29th, by which means I received it just a month before it was written. You do not find that I answer your questions to your satisfaction. Prove to me first that it was ever possible to answer anything to your satisfaction, so as that you would not grumble in half an hour. I am glad my writing puzzles you, for then your time will be employed in finding it out; and I am sure it costs me a great many thoughts to make my letters difficult. Sure Glass Heel is come over, and gave me a message from John Barber about the money on the jewels, which I shall answer. Malkin will be so glad to see Glass Heel — ay, Malkin. Yesterday I was half-way towards you, where I dined, and returned weary enough. I asked where that road to the left led, and they named the place. I wish your letters were as difficult as mine, for then they would be of no consequence, if they were dropped by careless messengers. A stroke thus — — — — signifies everything that may be said to Cad, at beginning or conclusion. It is I who ought to be in a huff that anything written by Cad should be difficult to Skinage. I must now leave off abruptly, for I intend to send this letter to-day. August 4th — — — — —

Glass Heel was the nickname the Van Homrighs used for their good friend, Charles Ford, with whom Swift had been very intimate in London. Ford had a handsome property near Dublin and is one of the few people who knew both Vanessa and Stella. The jewels referred to are almost certainly the diamond and pearl necklaces and earrings, which Mrs. Van Homrigh, in her will, bequeathed to her daughters, and which Vanessa had pledged to John Barber.

Swift's fear of his letters being opened leads to his invention of expressing his love by strokes. Vanessa's next letter, undated, but obviously a reply to the last, begins in an ecstasy:

Leabharlanna Átha Cliath

Celbridge, 1720

—. —, —, —, —, Cad —, you are good beyond expression, and I will never quarrel again if I can help it; but, with submission, 'tis you that are so hard to be pleased, though you complain of me. I thought the last letter I wrote to you was obscure and constrained enough: I took pains to write it after that manner. It would have been much easier for me to have wrote otherwise. I am not so unreasonable as to expect you should keep your word to a day, but six or seven days are great odds. Why should your apprehensions for Malkin hinder you from writing to me? I think you ought to have wrote the sooner to have comforted me. Malkin is better, but in a very weak way. Though those that saw me told you nothing of my illness, I do assure you I was for twenty-four hours as ill as 'twas possible to be, and live. You wrong me when you say I did not find that you answered my questions to my satisfaction. What I said was, I had asked those questions but could not find them answered to my satisfaction. How could they be answered in absence, since Somnus is not my friend? We have had a vast deal of thunder and lightning. Where do you think I wished to be then? And do you think that was the only time I wished so since I saw you? I am sorry my jealousy should hinder you from writing more love-letters, for I must chide sometimes, and I wish I could gain by it at this instant, as I have done and hope to do. Is my dating my letter wrong the only sign of my being in love? Pray tell me, did not you wish to come where that road to the left would have led you? I'm mightily pleased to hear you talk of being in a huff. 'Tis the first time you ever told me so. I wish I could see you in one. I am now as happy as I can be without seeing —, —, —, Cad. I beg you'll continue happiness to your own Skinage.

In spite of her attempts at obscurity, it is clear that, in Swift's absence, *questions* can only be satisfactorily answered in dreams; and Vanessa doesn't sleep. Thunder-storms remind her of Cad's protecting arms and of her constant desire to find herself there. She must chide, sometimes, for the joy of making up the quarrel, as she has done before and hopes to do again. She is as happy as she can ever be in the absence of —, —, —, *Cad*. She gladly admits his charge of being in love. It is the happy letter of a loving woman to a man who, she knows, loves her, too.

A few days later, Swift replies:

"*August* 12*th*, 1720.

I apprehended, on the return of the porter I sent with my last letter, that it would miscarry, because I saw the rogue was drunk; but yours made me easy. I must neither write to Malkin nor not write to her. You are like Lord Pembroke, who would neither go nor stay. Glass Heel talks of going to see you, and taking me with him, as he goes to his country house. I find you have company with you these two or three days: I hope they are diverting, at least to poor Malkin. Why should Cad's letters be difficult? I assure you — —'s are not at all.

I'm vexed that the weather hinders you from any pleasure in the country, because walking, I believe, would be of good use to you and Malkin. I reckon you will return a prodigious scholar, a most admirable nursekeeper, a perfect huswife and a great drinker of coffee. I have asked, and am assured there is not one beech in all your groves to carve a name on, nor a purling stream, for love or money, except a great river, which sometimes roars, but never murmurs — just like Governor Huff. We live here in a very dull Town, every valuable creature absent, and Cad — says he is weary of it, and would rather drink his coffee on the barrenest, highest mountain in Wales, than be King here.

A fig for partridges and quails;
Ye dainties, I know nothing of ye,
But on the highest mount in Wales
Would choose in peace to drink my coffee.

What would you give to have the history of Cad and —, exactly written, through all its steps, from the beginning to this time? I believe it would do well in verse, and be as long as the other. I hope it will be done. It ought to be an exact chronicle of twelve years, from the time of spilling the coffee to drinking coffee, from Dunstable to Dublin, with every single passage since. There would be the chapter of the blister; the chapter of Madam going to Kensington; the chapter of the Colonel's going to France; the chapter of the wedding, with the adventure of the lost key; of the strain; of the joyful return; two hundred chapters of madness; the chapter of long walks; the Berkshire surprise; fifty chapters of little times; the chapter of Chelsea; the chapter of swallow and cluster; a hundred whole books of myself and "so low"; the chapter of hide and whisper; the chapter of Who made it so? My sister's money. Cad bids me tell you, that if you complain of his puzzling you with difficult writing, he will give you enough of it.

See how much I have written without saying one word of Malkin, and you will be whipped before you deliver her a message with honour. I shall write to J. Barber next post, and desire him to be at no pains about his money; and I will take not one word of notice of his riches, on purpose to vex him. If Heaven had looked upon riches to be a valuable thing, it would not have given them to such a scoundrel. I delivered your enclosed letter to our friend, who happened to be with me when I received it. I find you are very much in his good graces; for he said a million of fine things upon it, though he would let nobody read a word of it but himself, though I was so

kind to shew him yours to me, as well as this, which he has laid a crown with me you will not understand — which is pretty odd for one that sets up for so high an opinion of your good sense.
I am ever, with the greatest truth, yours etc.
August 13.

Swift's attempts at *obscurity and constraint* were sufficient, no doubt, to mislead an untrustworthy messenger, but his letter can have offered little difficulty to the delighted eyes of Vanessa.

He was actually coming to Celbridge! . . . the visit she had dreamed about for six long years . . . he would see her home . . . she could show him her beautiful house, the fine pleasure-grounds sloping down to the lovely stretch of Liffey . . . Cad was coming, —, —, —, Cad. And, as if that news were not enough happiness for one letter to hold, he shows her that he has forgotten nothing of the past . . . reminds her of the times they have shared . . . tantalises her with the hope that he might even continue their own private history, *Cadenus and Vanessa.* He suggests chapter headings . . . Does she remember? Could she possibly forget?

To her shining eyes, each detail was as clear as noonday; but the dust of Time has blurred everything which it has not totally obliterated. Today the real significance lies in the fact that Swift, sharing Vanessa's memories, should have chosen to recall them to her. That so often remembered *coffee*, spilt years before in a Dunstable inn . . . *the Colonel*, her wild, young scamp of a brother . . . Swift had packed him off to France, with an introduction to his good friend, Prior, to get him away from mischief in London . . . and then the frantic apeals to his mother from a debtor's prison in Paris . . . poor, foolish Bartholomew, in his too early grave . . . These have left faint traces. But *the blister*? A clue lies, perhaps, in the circumstances surrounding Swift's fearful attack of shingles in London? *The wedding* . . . whose?

This memorable wedding, more fully described in a later letter as *the London Wedding,* was very probably that of Lady Mary Butler, younger daughter of the Duke of Ormond, who married Lord Ashburnham on the 20th October 1710. This young girl was a constant visitor at the Van Homrigh home and a close friend of Vanessa. In a letter from Swift to her cousin, Anne Long, he says of Vanessa (December 1711),

> *Her greatest favourites at present are Lady Ashburnham, her dog and myself.*

Both Swift and the Van Homrighs would certainly have been guests at this fashionable wedding. Swift describes Lord Ashburnham in the *Journal* as *the best match in England.* When she died a couple of years later, Swift wrote:

> *She was my greatest favourite, and I am in excessive concern for her loss.*

The strain . . . ? In a later letter, Swift expands this to *the strain by the box of books in London,* reminding her that, each time he changed lodgings, he invariably had a wooden-case of newly acquired books to be shifted and stored. *Chelsea* . . . ? That happy, happy time, when he came to see them twice a day, changing into his fine new wig and gown before going amongst the great . . . laughter in the Sluttery . . . fragrance of roasting oranges . . . the tang of strong, black coffee . . . O happy, happy Chelsea! . . . *The Berkshire Surprise*? He had been angry at first . . . . . . angry and embarrassed, when he looked up and saw her at the Vicarage gate . . . *Who* had seen her in the coach at Wantage? . . . *Whom* had she told she was coming? . . . *What* would the Reverend Mr. Geree suspect? . . . A stern sermon on his favourite subject, Discretion, and then, half-way through, she was in his arms . . . The happiness of being together again, even for a few short hours . . . And he ventures *a Crown* that she will not understand!

Swift, too, must have been in one of his rare completely happy moods when he wrote that letter. It bubbles with gaiety. Even his good, faithful friend, John Barber, becomes *a scoundrel*, and he invents yet another personality for himself, *our friend*, to whom he delivers Vanessa's letter, *I find you are very much in his good graces, for he said a million of fine things upon it. . . . So low*, his pet name for her when she moped. . . .

People of Vanessa's temperament tend to swing between the heights of joy and the depths of despair. On the 13th August 1720, as she read that letter, she must have spent some hours on a sunbathed peak. Her ardent joy fills her immediate reply:

Celbridge, 1720.

-, -, -, *Cad, is it possible you will come and see me? I beg for God sake you will. I would give all world to see you here, and Malkin would be extremely happy. Do you think the time long since I saw you? I did design seeing you this week, but will not stir, in hopes of your coming here. I beg you'll write two or three words by the bearer, to let me know if you think you'll come this week: I shall have the note tonight. You make me happy beyond expression by your goodness. It would be too much once to hope for such a history. If you had laid a thousand pounds that I should not understand your letter, you had lost it. Tell me sincerely, did those circumstances crowd on you, or did you recollect them to make me happy?*

Her messenger was to wait for his answer. There is no record of that visit to Celbridge. The only thing of note in the letter is that it shows that she was in the habit of visiting Dublin, from time to time, and seeing him there. Presumably the country air of Celbridge was considered better for her dying sister, and so they had to stay there.

The next surviving letter is from Swift, and there is a gap of two months between it and the last:

October 15th 1720.
I sit down with the first opportunity I have to write to you; and the Lord knows when I can find conveniency to send this letter; for all the morning I am plagued with impertinent visits, or impertinent business, below any man of sense or honour to endure, if it were in any way avoidable. Dinners and afternoons and evenings are spent abroad and in walking, to help and avoid spleen, so far as I can; so that when I am not so good a correspondent as I could wish, you are not to quarrel and be Governor, but to impute it to my situation, and to conclude infallibly that I have the same respect, esteem and kindness for you I ever professed to have and shall ever preserve, because you will always merit the utmost that can be given you—especially if you go on to read, and still further improve your mind and the talents nature has given you. I had a letter from your friend, John Barber, in London, in answer to what I told you Glass-heel said about the money. J. B.'s answer is that you are a person of honour, that you need give yourself no trouble about it, that you will pay when you are able, and he shall be content until then. Those are his very words; and you see he talks in the style of a rich man, though terribly pulled down by the fall of stocks. I am glad you did not sell your annuities, unless somebody were to manage and transfer them while stocks were high. I am in much concern for poor Malkin and the more because I am sure you are too. You ought to be as cheerful as you can, for both your sakes, and read pleasant things that will make you laugh, and not sit moping with your elbows on your knees on a little stool at the fire. It is most

infallible that riding would do Malkin much more good than any other thing, provided fair days and warm clothes be provided; and so it would to you; and if you lose any skin, you know Job says: Skin for skin will a man give for his life. It is either Job or Satan says so, for aught you know.

October 17*th—I had not a moment to finish this since I sat down to it. A person was with me just now, and interrupted me as I was going on with telling me of great people here losing their places; and now some more are coming about business, so adieu till by and by or to-morrow.*

October 18*th—I am getting an ill head in this cursed town, for want of exercise. I wish I were to walk with you fifty times about your garden, and then—drink your coffee. I was sitting last night with half a score of both sexes for an hour, and grew as weary as a dog. Glass Heel takes up abundance of my time, in spite of my teeth; everybody grows silly and disagreeable, or I grow monkish and spleenatic, which is the same thing. Conversation is full of nothing but South Sea, and the ruin of the Kingdom, and scarcity of money. I had a thousand times rather hear the Governor chide two hours without reason.*

October 20*th—The Governor was with me at six o'clock this morning, but did not stay two minutes, and deserves a chiding, which you must give when you drink your coffee next. I hope to send this letter to-morrow. I am a good deal out of order in my head after a little journey I made, and ate too much, I suppose, or travelling in a coach after it. I am now sitting alone, and will go write Malkin. So adieu — — — — —.*

In this letter, he warmly advocates his cure-all for ill-health—exercise; horse-riding will help even poor Malkin, apparently in the last stages of tuberculosis. All through

Swift's life, he exercised himself mercilessly, from the early days when he used to run up a hill at Moor Park, to those darker days towards the end, when in wet weather, he used to rush up and down the Deanery stairs, until he calculated that he had covered ten miles. In 1720, his ill health was increasing, his attacks of Meniere's disease were more frequent and its giddy spells left him ever more shaken and depressed. Ill and weary, he wishes he could leave *this cursed town* and take refuge with her in the quiet Celbridge garden, walking around it fifty times, *and then—drink your coffee.* Many people have speculated as to what the words mean. What Vanessa understood by the phrase is one of the many secrets in this strange adventure in love.

Dublin can talk of nothing but the bursting of the South Sea Bubble; rather than listen to the wearisome talk, he would willingly be chided by Vanessa for two hours on end, even though he didn't deserve to be scolded. And then, next day, he adds a postscript to tell her that he has been dreaming about her, in the early hours; that the dream was too brief and that there would be reproaches *when next she drank her coffee.* He ends this touching letter with no less than seven strokes, each one a warrant for the most loving words she cares to substitute.

When Swift wrote this letter, he was almost fifty-three and Vanessa was thirty one. They had known one another for some fourteen years, through good times and bad, and they had arrived at a relationship which this letter makes clear.

The next, dated merely 1720, is from Vanessa:

Celbridge.
You had heard from me before, but that my messenger was not to be had till today; and now I have only time to thank you for yours, because he is going about his business this moment, which is very happy for you, or you would

have had a long letter full of spleen. Never was human creature more distressed than I have been since I came. Poor Malkin has had two or three relapses, and is in so bad a way that I fear she will never recover. Judge now what a way I am in, absent from you and loaded with melancholy on her score. I have been very ill with a stitch in my side, which is not very well yet.

Her next letter, also is dated:

Celbridge 1720.

Believe me 'tis with the utmost regret that I now complain to you, because I know your good nature, such that you cannot see any human being miserable without being sensibly touched. Yet what can I do? I must either unload my heart and tell you all my griefs, or sink under the unexpressible distress I now suffer by your prodigious neglect of me. 'Tis now ten long weeks since I saw you, and in all that time I have never received but one letter from you and a little note, with an excuse. Oh —, —, —, how have you forgot me! You endeavour by severities to force me from you; nor can I blame you, for with the utmost distress and confusion, I behold myself the cause of uneasy reflections to you. Yet I cannot comfort you, but here declare that 'tis not in the power of art, time or accident to lessen the unexpressible passion, which I have for -, -, -. Put my passion under the utmost restraint, send me as distant from you as the earth will allow, yet you cannot banish those charming ideas, which will ever stick by me, whilst I have the use of memory. Nor is the love I bear you only seated in my soul, for there is not a single atom of my frame that is not blended with it. Therefore, don't flatter yourself that separation will ever change my sentiments, for I find myself unquiet in the midst of silence, and my heart is at once pierced by sorrow and love. For Heaven's sake, tell me what caused this prodigious change in you, which I have found of late. If you have the least remains of pity for me left, tell me tenderly. No, don't tell it, so that it may cause my present death; and don't suffer me to live a life like a languishing death, which is the only life I can lead, if you have lost any of your tenderness for me.

Ill herself, and worn out with the care of her dying sister, Vanessa is driven, by some unexplained break, to a depth of misery and despair, out of which rises her poignant cry *I find myself unquiet in the midst of silence, and my heart is at once pierced by sorrow and love.* Both as an artist and as a lover, Swift must have envied her that phrase.

Her next letter, which also bears the date 1720, is written in the same despairing mood:

Celbridge 1720.

Tell me sincerely if you have once wished with earnestness to see me since I wrote to you. No, so far from that, you have not once pitied me, though I told you how I was distressed. Solitude is insupportable to a mind which is not easy. I have worn out my days in sighing, and my nights with watching and thinking of -, -, -, -, -, -, who thinks not of me. How many letters must I send before I shall receive an answer? Can you deny me, in my misery, the only comfort which I can expect at present? Oh! that I could hope to see you here, or that I could go to you. I was born with violent passions, which terminate all in one —that unexpressible passion I have for you. Consider the killing emotions which I feel from your neglect of me, or I shall lose my senses. Sure, you cannot possibly be so much taken up but you might command a moment to write to me, and force your inclinations to do so great a charity.

I firmly believe, could I know your thoughts (which no human creature is capable of guessing at, because never anyone living thought like you), I should find that you have often, in a rage, wished me religious, hoping then I should have paid my devotions to Heaven. But that would not spare you, for was I an enthusiast, still you'd be the deity I should worship. What marks are there of a deity but what you are known by? You are present everywhere; your dear image is always before my eyes; sometimes you strike me with that prodigious awe I tremble with fear; at other times, a charming compassion shines through your countenance, which revives my soul. Is it not more reasonable to adore a radiant form seen, than one only described?

Vanessa is spending her nights watching beside her sister's sickbed, her days in the cold, bleak, winter climate of Celbridge, listening to the river storming through her gardens, the wind howling in the trees. She is herself sick, in body and in mind, deserted by her God. There is no explanation of Swift's apparent neglect of her. But, somewhere during this period, he was writing his masterpiece, *Gulliver,* and the genius that drove him into immortality may have dealt ruthlessly with mere human needs. His next letter to Vanessa is a short one, almost surely delivered by hand at her Dublin home:

To Mrs. Esthr. Va.

I am surprised and grieved beyond what I can express. I read your letter twice before I knew what it meant, nor can I yet well believe my eyes. Is that poor good creature dead? I observed she looked a little ghastly on Saturday, but it is against the usual way for one in her case to die so sudden. In God's sake get your friends about you, to advise and to order everything in the forms. It is all you have to do. I want comfort myself in this case, and can give little. Time alone must give it to you. Nothing now is your part but decency. I was wholly unprepared against so sudden an event, and pity you most of all creatures at present. — *Monday.*

It would seem that, when her case was hopeless, Mary Van Homrigh may have been moved back to Dublin, where medical help would have been more easily available. This note was written on the day she died, and Swift had apparently visited her two days before. She was buried, near her father, on 3rd March 1720-21, in St. Andrew's Church. Swift's letter is a curious mixture of genuine sorrow for the girl's death and an obvious fear lest, in her emotional crisis, Vanessa should in any way publicly involve *him*. He implores her to rely entirely for advice and assistance on her *friends*, making it quite clear that he (who was, at the least, her best and oldest friend) was not available. It would be revealing to know whether his discretion kept him away from St. Andrew's Church, when Vanessa, the last of the Van Homrighs, stood beside poor Malkin's grave, or whether fear of the watchful eyes in *this cursed town* held him within the Deanery walls.

With her sister's death, Vanessa became a completely free agent. Presumably, she now spent most of her time in Dublin, saw Swift frequently and had no need of letters. One short note, from Swift, is addressed to

> *Mrs. Esth. Vanhomrigh. June 1st.*
> -, -, -, -, -, -, -, *I cannot contrive to get this catalogue copied out, and therefore have delivered it to Mr. Worrall for you, and told him it was some papers directed to me for you from England. Pray God protect you. Adieu.*

Once again, there are seven dashes to be filled in with whatever words of love she pleases. Mr. Worrall was his Vicar at St. Patrick's who did much confidential business for the Dean. The reference to the catalogue may be explained by an allusion in one of Doctor Berkeley's letters to Prior, some years later, in which he states that, after Vanessa's death, he had seen a *catalogue of her debts clearly stated, drawn up by her order.*

The next letter is written by Swift:

July 5th 1721 *Gaulstown, near Kinnegad.*
It was not convenient, hardly possible, to write to you before now, though I had a more than ordinary desire to do it, considering the disposition I found you in last; though I hope I left you in a better. I must here beg you to take more care of your health, by company and exercise; or else the spleen will get the better of you, than which there is not a more foolish or troublesome disease; and what you have no pretences in the world to, if all the advantages of life can be any defence against it. Cad - assures me he continues to esteem and love and value you above all things, and so will do to the end of his life, but at the same time entreats that you will not make yourself or him unhappy by imaginations. The wisest men of all ages have thought it the best course to seize the minutes as they fly, and to make every innocent action an amusement. If you knew how I struggle for a little health, what uneasiness I am at in riding and walking, and refraining from everything agreeable to my taste, you would think it but a small thing to take a coach now and then, and to converse with fools or impertinents, to avoid spleen and sickness. Without health, you will lose all desire of drinking your coffee, and so low as to have no spirits.
I answer all your questions that you were used to ask Cad -, and he protests he answers them, in the affirmative. How go your affairs? You were once a good lawyer, but Cad - hath spoiled you. I had a weary journey in an Irish stage-coach, but am pretty well since. Pray write to me cheerfully, without complaints or expostulations, or else Cad - shall know it and punish you.
What is this world, without being as easy in it as prudence and fortune can make it? I find it every day more silly and insignificant, and I conform myself to it for my own

ease. I am here as deep employed in other folks' plantations and ditchings as if they were my own concern, and think of my absent friends with delight, and hopes of seeing them happy and of being happy with them. Shall you, who have so much honour and good sense, act otherwise, to make Cad - and yourself miserable? Settle your affairs, and quit this scoundrel island, and things will be as you desire.

I can say no more, being called away, mais soyez assurée que jamais personne du monde a étè aimée, honorée, estimée, adorée par votre ami que vous. I drank no coffee since I left you, nor intend to till I see you again. There is none worth drinking but yours, if myself may be the judge.

Rest assured that you are the only person on earth who has ever been loved, honoured, esteemed, adored by your friend. Swift could scarcely have made a clearer declaration of his love, and it must either be accepted as a genuine expression of his emotions (after an acquaintance of fourteen years), or else as a despicable lie from an elderly hypocrite.

This is the only surviving letter which was undoubtedly written during the year 1721; it came from the fine Meath estate of Swift's friend, Chief Baron Rochford. His visit there was, it seems, planned to last a couple of months, and the impending separation probably accounts for the mood in which he had found Vanessa, and which he hoped he had improved before he left her. Once again, he urges her to take exercise and go into company. He himself, as he writes to the Archbishop a few days later, is *rowing after health like a waterman and riding after it like a postboy*. He is also deeply interested *in other folks' plantations and ditching, as if they were my own affair*. Swift could never resist such activities; of the garden he made in Dublin there is scarcely a trace, and at Laracor, only his willows survive, straggling along his well-loved *Canal* and the River Walk.

It would be interesting to know what company he urges her to keep, for the names of few of her friends survive, and they mostly in her will. Near Celbridge, there were Mr. and Mrs. George Finey, to whose son, poor Malkin's godson, she left £25. To Mrs. Finey and her sister, she left money for mourning, so that they may have been connections. She only mentions one relative, *the Reverend Mr. John Antrobus my cousin*, to whom she left money for a ring. There is no way of knowing who were the *fools or impertinents*, whom she was to take a coach and visit.

Poor Vanessa's legal affairs were still in such an inextricable tangle, in spite of all her efforts, that she must often have been reduced to despair, her brother's and sister's estates being now added to the muddle. Nevertheless, Swift assures her that she enjoys *all the advantages of life.* Swift's injunction to settle her affairs and leave this *scoundrel island* must have produced, at best, a wry smile.Only Vanessa could have told the meaning of his next words, *and things will be as you desire.* About this time, it is probable that Swift had begun to consider the possibility of re-establishing himself in the English scene. Seven years of absence is a long time, and even the most virulent political feuds die away. Besides, Swift must have been well aware that, with the publication of *Gulliver*, he had a brilliant chance of real literary fame; and it seems that MSS. copies were being discreetly circulated. A little later, Lord Bolingbroke wrote to him, *I long to see your Travels;* and Swift wrote to his good friend, Pope, pointing out that there was now no reason why he should not be treated, with *at least tolerable quarter*, by the ruling Whigs. Vanessa would have been well aware of such plans, and needed only Swift's reminder that he hoped very soon to be back in England, for most of his time, with her and his old friends. How gladly she would have left *this scoundrel island*, where no seclusion could protect her from rumours of *the Ladies*, around whom so much of the Deanery social life revolved. The shadow of Esther Johnson, even as an old friend of Swift's youth, must often have fallen, dark, across Vanessa's moods; even had Swift quoted to her his recent lines on Stella, *But her graceful black locks were all mingled with grey.*

In almost a year, there is no existing letter, and then Swift writes from,

> *Clogher, June* 1*st* 1722.
> *This is the first time I have set pen to paper since I left Dublin, having not been in any settled place till ten days ago, and I missed one post by ignorance, and that stopped me five days. Before that time, I was much out of order, by usual consequences of wet weather and change of drink; neither am I yet established, though much better than I was. The weather has been so constantly bad that I wanted all the healthy advantages of the country, and seems likely to continue so. It would have been infinitely better once a week to have met Kendall and so forth, where one might pass three or four hours in drinking coffee in the morning, or dining tête-à-tête, and drinking coffee again till seven. I answer all the questions you can ask me in the affirmative. I remember your detesting and despising the conversations of the world. I have been so mortified with a man and his lady here two days, that it has made me as peevish as—I want a comparison. I hope you have gone or are going to your country seat, though I think you have a term upon your hands. I shall be here long enough to receive your answer, and perhaps to write to you again; but then I shall go further off (if my health continues) and shall let you know my stages. I have been for some days as spleenatic as ever you were in your life, which is a bold word. Remember I still enjoin you reading and exercise for the improvement of your mind and health of your body, and grow less romantic and talk and act like*

a man of this world. It is the saying of the world, and I believe you often say, I love myself; but I am so low, I cannot say it, though your new acquaintance were with you, which I heartily wish, for the sake of you and myself. God send you through your law and your reference; and remember that riches are nine parts in ten of all that is good in life, and health is the tenth. Drinking coffee comes long after, and yet it is the eleventh; but without the two former you cannot drink it right; and remember the china in the old house, and Ryder Street, and the Colonel's journey to France, and the London Wedding, and the sick lady at Windsor, and the strain by the box of books at London. Last year, I writ you civilities, and you were angry; this year, I will write you none, and you will be angry, yet my thoughts were still the same, and I give you leave to be the carver, and will be answerable for them. I hope you will let me have some of your money when I see you, which I will pay you honestly again. Repondez-moy si vous entendez bien tout cela, et croyez que je seray toujours tout ce que vous desirez. Adieu.

In this highly enigmatic letter, Swift once again reminds her of the high points of their past; but gives no clue which might identify the anniversary he refers to, *this* year, without last year's civilities.

The most significant reminder, however, begins, *It would have been infinitely better once a week to have met Kendall, and so forth, where one might pass three or four hours in drinking coffee in the morning, or dining* tête-à-tête *and drinking coffee again till seven.* Almost exactly two months later, he expands this: *The same scene has passed forty times . . . yet each has* ses agréments particuliers.

According to the City Records, a Thomas Kendall became a Freeman of Dublin, in 1749. In his will, he is described as a bookbinder. He lived in St. Andrew's Parish, as did

Vanessa; he married a woman named Anne M'Loghlin. It is quite clear that *someone* named Kendall provided a place where they could meet, weekly and regularly; this bookbinder may well have been the man. The many commentators who have brushed aside the relationship of Swift and Vanessa—a relationship now in its seventeenth and last year—as one in which an importunate woman harassed an indifferent man, have chosen to ignore Swift's own statement that they met regularly, once a week, over a long period. These meetings took place as the other letter specifies *at ten in the morning*, when they passed *three or four hours*, and sometimes *from two till seven*, each having *its particular pleasures*. (Once again the difficulty arises as to the real significance of coffee-drinking and of the ritual asking and answering of Vanessa's *questions*. Whatever be the solution, it is quite obvious that the words do not mean precisely what they appear to say.) And, although Swift assures her that *riches are nine parts in ten of all that is good in life, drinking coffee comes long after, and yet is the eleventh; but without riches and health, you cannot drink it right*, it is clear that Swift, who had thrown discretion to the winds of Dublin by meeting Vanessa weekly and regularly, must still have been very deeply in love with her: It would seem that such meetings, often involving a *tête-à-tête* dinner, must have required an extremely discreet and trustworthy host; and it is perhaps another minute piece missing from the puzzle, that the host should be closely connected with a family named M'Loghlin. Of this, more later.

The phrase, *my thoughts are still the same and I give you leave to be the carver and will be answerable for them* has puzzled editors, but Swift—as so often—provides his own answer in a poem . . .

To a Lady, who desired the author to write some Verses for her.

You must learn, if you would gain us
With good sense to entertain us.
Scholars, when good sense describing
Call it tasting and imbibing;
Metaphoric meat and drink
Is to understand and think;
We may *carve* for others thus
And let others carve for us;
To discourse and to attend
Is to *help* yourself and friend.
Conversation is but *carving*,
Carve for all, yourself is starving;
Give no more to ev'ry guest
Then he's able to digest;
Give him always of the prime,
And but little at a time.
Carve to all, but just enough;
Let them neither starve nor stuff;
And, that you may have your due
Let your neighbours *carve* for you.

The italics are Swift's.

His final request for the loan of her money when next he saw her—she was always in financial straits and he was a relatively wealthy man— must obviously be classed amongst the group of things which do not mean what is, apparently, said. To stress that, he adds his query in French, ending with the assurance that he will always be everything she can wish.

Vanessa's next letter, undated, but almost certainly an answer to the last, is written from her Dublin house:

-, -, -, *Cad, I thought you had quite forgot both me and your promise of writing to me. Was it not very unkind to be five weeks absent, without sending me one line to let me know you were well and remembered me? Besides, you have had such bad weather that you could have no diversion abroad. What then could you do but write and read? I know you do not love cards, neither is this a time of year for that amusement. Since I saw you, I have gone more into this world that I did for some time past, because you commanded me; and I do here protest that I am more and more sick of it every day than other. One day this week, I was to visit a great lady that has been a-travelling for some time past, where I found a very great assembly of ladies and beaux, dressed (as I suppose) to a nicety. I hope you'll pardon me now, if I tell you that I heartily wished you a spectator; for I very much question if in your life you ever saw the like scene or one more extraordinary. The lady's behaviour was blended with so many different characters, I cannot possibly describe it, without tiring your patience. But the audience seemed to me a creation of her own, they were so very obsequious. Their forms and gestures were very like those of baboons or monkeys. They all grinned and chattered at the same time, and that of things I did not understand. The room being hung with arras, in which were trees, very well described, just as I was considering their beauty, and wishing myself in the country with -, -, -, one of these animals snatched my fan and was so pleased with me, that it seized me with such a panic, that I apprehended nothing less than being carried up to the top of the house, and served as a friend of yours was; but in this, one of their own species came in upon which they all began to make their grimaces; which opportunity I took, and made my escape.*

I have not made one single step, either in law or reference since I saw you. I meet with nothing but disappointments, yet I am obliged to stay in Town attending on Mr. Partinton, etc. which is very hard. I do declare I have so little joy in life, that I don't care how soon mine ends. For God's sake, write to me soon and kindly, for in your absence your letters are all the joy I have on earth; and sure you are too good-natured to grudge one hour in a week to make any human creature happy. -, -, -, -, Cad, think of me and pity me.

Clearly, what with the weather, her failing health, her social life, her executor, Mr. Partinton and her absence from Swift, poor Vanessa was *so low.* It would be interesting to know the identity of the much-travelled *great lady.* The most significant item in this letter is her allusion to an incident in *Gulliver's Voyage to Brobdingnag,* in which he is carried off by a monkey. This reference shows that she had either been shown the MSS, or had discussed the work with Swift. It was not published for more than four years afterwards. There is also internal evidence that Vanessa was shown the MSS of *Gulliver's Voyages to Lilliput* and that some words in the Lilliputian *language* contain private jokes between herself and Swift. Otherwise, it is difficult to account for the very first words Gulliver hears fram a Lilliputian, who *lifting up his hands and eyes by way of admiration cried out, Hekinah degul*! Swift had a habit of conferring pet-names, and amongst those which he gave to Vanessa—itself a name which he invented for her—was Heskinage. It is impossible to believe that when he wrote those two words, which include every letter of that very curious name except one, he did so by accident. As is well known, Swift had always had a passion for playing with words; cyphers, puns and anagrams constantly appear in his work. It would indeed be very remarkable if he had resisted the temptation when inventing new *languages.* The word *hurgo,* which he assures us, is Lilliputian for *a great Lord,* looks suspiciously like an anagram for *rogue;* and the shameful antics of the courtiers are described as *a summerset,* a name Swift could not possibly have written without remembering his bitter enemy, the Duchess. Perhaps someone will decipher the *languages* in

Gulliver's travels. So far as Vanessa is concerned, they are only important in so far as they appear to show how intimately she was associated with Swift's masterpiece.

Swift was still on his country tour when he wrote the next letter.

To Mrs. Vanhomrigh,

Lough-Gall, County of Armagh. July 13*th* 1722

I received yours, and have changed places so often since that I could not assign a place where I might expect an answer from—; and if you be now in the country, and this letter does not reach you in due time after the date, I shall not expect to hear from you, because I leave this place the beginning of August. I am well pleased with the account of your visit and the behaviour of the ladies. I see every day as silly things among both sexes, and yet endure them for the sake of amusements. The worst thing in you and me is that we are too hard to please, and whether we have not made ourselves so, is the question. At least, I believe we have the same reason. One thing I differ from you in, that I do not quarrel with my best friends. I believe you have ten angry passages in your letter, and every one of them enough to spoil two days apiece of riding and walking. We differ prodigiously in one point: I fly from the spleen to the world's end, you run out of your way to meet it. I doubt the bad weather has hindered you much from the diversions of your country house, and put you upon thinking in your chamber. The use I have made of it was to read I know not how many diverting books of history and travels.

I wish you would get yourself a horse, and have always two servants to attend you, and visit your neighbours, the worse the better. There is a pleasure in being reverenced, and that is always in your powers, by your superiority of sense and an easy fortune. The best maxim I know in this

life, is to drink your coffee when you can, and when you cannot, to be easy without it. While you continue to be spleenatic, count upon it I will always preach. Thus much I sympathise with you, that I am not cheerful enough to write, for I believe coffee once a week is necessary to that. I can sincerely answer all your questions as I used to do; but then I give all possible way to amusements, because they preserve my temper as exercise does my health; and without health and good humour I had rather be a dog. I have shifted scenes oftener that I ever did in my life, and I believe have lain in thirty beds since I left town, and always drew up the clothes with my left hand, which is a superstition I have learned these ten years.
These country posts are always so capricious that we are forced to send our letters at a call, on a sudden; and mine is now demanded, though it goes not out till to-morrow. Be cheerful, and read and ride and laugh, as Cad - used to advise you long ago. I hope your affairs are on some better settlement. I long to see you in figure and equipage; pray do not lose that taste. Farewell.

Here once again are the mysterious allusions to the drinking of coffee and the answering of questions; but this time he tells her (reminding her of *Kendall*), that, in order to be cheerful it is necessary to drink coffee once a week. Presumably, the fact that he had learned a superstition about strange beds in 1712 also revived some mutual memory.

The next letter is the last which has survived from Vanessa to Swift. It is a reply to his letter of the 13th July, and is probably written during that month.

-, -, -, Cad, I am and cannot avoid being in the spleen to the last degree. Everything combines to make me so. Is it not very hard to have so good a fortune as I have and yet no more command of that fortune than if I had no title to it? One of the Doctors is—I don't know what

to call him. He behaved so abominably to me the other day that, had I been a man he should have heard more of it. In short, he does nothing but trifle and make excuses. I really believe he heartily repents that he ever undertook it, since he heard counsel first plead, finding his friend more in the wrong than he imagined. Here am I, obliged to stay in this odious town, attending and losing my health and humour. Yet this and all other disappointments in life I can bear with ease, but that of being neglected by -, -, -, Cad. He has often told me that the best maxim in life, and always held by the wisest of all ages, is to seize the moments as they fly; but those happy moments always fly out of the reach of the unfortunate. Pray tell -, -, -, Cad I don't remember any angry passages in my letter, and am very sorry if they appeared so to him. Spleen, I cannot help, so you must excuse it. I do all I can to get the better of it and it is too strong for me.
I have read more since I saw Cad than I did in a great while past, and chose those books that required most attention, on purpose to engage my thoughts; but, I find the more I think the more unhappy I am. I had once a mind not to have wrote to you, for fear of making you uneasy to find me so dull, but I could not keep to that resolution. For the pleasure of writing to you, the satisfaction I have in your remembering me, and the delight I have in expecting one from -, -, -, Cad, makes me rather choose to give you some uneasiness than to add to my own.

She is still hopelessly embroiled with law and lawyers, forced to remain in *this odious town*, ill, depressed and, above all her other miseries, absent from Swift. In that state of mind, Vanessa vanishes into a void. In ten months, she is dead, aged thirty-four.

The correspondence ends with a last letter from Swift, *To Mrs. Vanhomry, August 7th*, 1722.

I am this hour leaving my present residence, and if I fix anywhere, shall let you know it; for I fain would wait till I get a little good weather for riding and walking, there never having been such a season as this remembered; though I doubt you know nothing of it but what you learn by sometimes looking out at your back windows to call your people. I had your last, with a spleenatic account of your law affairs. You were once a better solicitor, when you could contrive to make others desire your consent to an Act of Parliament against their own interest, to advance yours. Yet at present, you want neither power, nor skill, but disdain to exercise either. When you are melancholy, read diverting or amusing books: it is my receipt, and seldom fails. Health, good humour and fortune are all that is valuable in this life, and the last contributes to the two former.

I have not rode in all above four hundred miles since I saw you, nor do I believe I shall ride above two hundred more till I see you again. But I desire you will not venture to shake me by the hand; for I am in mortal fear of the itch, and have no hope left, but that some ugly vermin called ticks have got into my skin, of which I have pulled out some and must scratch out the rest. Is not this enough to give one the spleen? For I doubt no Christian family will receive me. And this is all a man gets by a northern journey. It would be unhappy for me to be as nice in my conversation and company as you are, which is the only thing wherein you agree with Glass-heel, who declares there is not a conversable creature in Ireland except Cad -. What would you do in these parts, where politeness is as much a stranger as cleanliness?

I am stopped, and this letter is intended to travel with me, so Adieu till the next stage.

August 8th. Yesterday, I rode twentyeight miles without being weary, and I wish little Heskinage could do as much.

Here I leave this letter to travel one way, while I go another, but where I do not know, nor what cabins or bogs are in my way.

I see you, this moment, as you are visible at ten o'clock in the morning; and now you are asking your questions round, and I am answering them, with a great deal of affected delays; and the same scene has passed forty times as well as the other from two till seven, longer than the first by two hours, yet each has ses agremens particuliers. *A long vacation, law lies asleep, and bad weather: how do you wear away your time? Is it among the fields and groves of your country seat, or among your cousins in Town, or thinking in a strain that will be sure to vex you, and then reasoning and forming teasing conclusions from mistaken thoughts? The best companion for you is a philosopher, whom you would regard as much as a sermon. I have read more trash since I left you than would fill all your shelves, and am abundantly the better for it, though I scarce remember a syllable.*

Go over the scenes of Windsor, Cleveland Row, Ryder Street, St. James's, Kensington, the Sluttery, the Colonel in France etc. Cad thinks often of these, especially on horseback, as I am assured. What a foolish thing is Time, and how foolish is man, who would be as angry if Time stopped as if it passed. But I will not proceed at this rate, for I am fast writing myself into the spleen, which is the only thing I would not compliment you by imitating. So adieu till the next place I fix in, if I fix at all till I return, and that I leave to fortune and the weather.

His reference here to the circumstances leading up to the Act of Parliament has already been commented on; no one can doubt that Swift had full knowledge of them.

In spite of bad weather, he is still dogged by the necessity of exercising to improve his health. Fully conscious that his lengthy absence is greatly aggravating her increasing melancholia, he tries to lighten it by reminding her of their weekly meetings, with the questions and answers—*the same scene has passed forty times, as well as the other,* each with its *special pleasures.* For the third time, he recalls the incidents of their past; and in this last surviving letter, he returns, appropriately, to their beginnings, to *the Sluttery, which I have so often found to be the most agreeable chamber in the world.*

IX

THERE follow months of unbroken silence. On the 8th August, 1722, Swift wrote his last letter, reminding Vanessa fondly of their weekly *rendezvous* and holding out hope of seeing her soon; on the 1st May, 1723, she made her last will, leaving the bulk of her considerable property to strangers and pointedly omitting the name of Jonathan Swift. There is no reliable account of what happened between these two dates, but there is a general agreement that *something* did—something so terrible that it hastened Vanessa's death and also caused a complete break between Stella and Swift. The Reverend Dr. Delany, intimate friend of both, says,

> *I have good reason to believe that they both were greatly shocked and distressed (tho' it may be differently) upon the occasion.*

Various explanations have been suggested by other contemporary writers. Lord Orrery states that Vanessa wrote to Swift, proposing marriage and that Swift rejected her. Deane Swift says that her unrequited passion was the remote cause of her death, as *Dr. Swift never once made her the most distant overtures of marriage.* He adds, that she only heard that Swift was married to Stella a couple of months before her death. Dr. Delany suggests that the situation was complicated by the fact that, as he delicately put it, *she certainly gave herself up (as Ariadne did) to Bacchus, from the day she was deserted.* The most widespread version is that Vanessa wrote a letter, either to Stella or Swift, asking whether they were married; that Swift rode immediately to Celbridge, threw down her letter in a black fury, and rode away, for ever.

Only conjectures fill the gap, between the 8th August, 1722, and the end of April, 1723, and no very satisfactory conjecture has yet been produced. The suggestion that this three-fold rupture was caused by an enquiry as to whether Swift and Stella were married is not a reasonable one.

These two women had, for some nine years, been living in the small circle of Dublin society. The miraculous thing is that they seem to have managed never to meet; they had at least three friends in common, Archbishop King, Dr. Pratt, Provost of Trinity, and Charles Ford...*Glass Heel* to the Van Homrighs, *Don Carlos* to the Ladies. For nine years, Stella's friends had been constantly speculating about a possible marriage between her and the Dean. (This speculation continues to this day.) If Vanessa did, finally, demand an answer to this over-due question, it is conceivable that, having since 1711 regarded herself as Swift's affianced wife, she might well have felt outraged had she been told that he and Stella *were* married. Such a shocking betrayal would very reasonably account for Vanessa's subsequent anger; for the new will, the instructions for publication of her papers and her death within a few weeks.

But this explanation does not account for the extraordinary behaviour of Stella and the Dean. To quote their mutual good friend, Dr. Delany, again:

I have good reason to believe that they both were greatly shocked and distressed (tho' it may be differently) upon this occasion. The Dean made a tour to the South of Ireland for about two months, at this time, to dissipate his thoughts and give place to obloquy. And Stella retired (upon the earnest invitation of the owner) to the house of a cheerful, generous, good-natured friend of the Dean's whom she also much loved and honoured. There my informant often saw her and, I have reason to believe, used his utmost endeavour to relieve, support and amuse her in this sad situation.

Dr. Delany, being himself *my informant*, had every opportunity of observing Stella's shocked and distressed condition, during the six months she spent at Charles Ford's sheltering house, where he did his utmost to relieve her *sad situation*.

Surely the condition he pictures is a very exaggeratedly tragic one for a woman who had merely been asked whether she were married? And what *obloquy* was the Dean escaping from? Had Vanessa written to ask Stella whether she were the Dean's wife, she might very well have been annoyed, particularly if she could not answer in the affirmative. Had Vanessa written her query to Swift, he *might* have flown into one of his furies — unreasonably, since over the years he must often have discussed his relationship with Stella, recognising that Vanessa had a perfect right to know where he stood between the two women. But his angers were transient, and such an incident could not account for his subsequent behaviour.

Immediately after Swift's dramatic break with Vanessa, Stella and her companion, Mrs. Dingley, fled from Dublin —rumour says without seeing the Dean—taking refuge at Wood Park, where they remained for over six months, without ever setting foot in Dublin, some ten miles distant. There, they were *relieved and supported* in their *sad situation* by their circle of friends, headed by Dr. Sheridan and Dr. Delany. Swift, who apparently did *not* visit them, remained in Dublin during the few weeks while Vanessa was dying, probably in her house in Turnstile Alley. *What* he feared would happen at her death is not known; that he *did* fear something is obvious, and the town was probably buzzing with speculations about the dying woman. The proof of his apprehensions of a shattering scandal is the letter he wrote, at midnight, to his friend Knightley Chetwode, on the day Vanessa died,

2nd June, 1723 — past twelve at night . . . I am forced to leave this town sooner than I expected . . .

On 4th June, Vanessa was buried, near her father and her sister, in St. Andrew's Church. Swift was not at the funeral; he had left Dublin the previous day, according to Dr. Sheridan, leaving no address, so that not even the clergy of his own Cathedral could contact him. Weeks passed, and they were extremely worried, until in August he wrote to Dr. Sheridan, saying that he proposed returning some weeks later. In that letter he asked, *Are the Ladies in town, or in the country? If I knew I would write to them. Are they in health?*

So the break between the unhappy Ladies and the fugitive Dean had been complete.

Since none of the proffered explanations can be held to account reasonably for these happenings, there is at least room for another conjecture which might better explain the disaster which overtook these three unhappy people. The known facts give support to the following theory.

By the Spring of 1723, Vanessa must have been far advanced in tuberculosis, and forced to realise by the tragically early deaths of her brothers and sister that she, too, was doomed. All her life, she had been an easy prey to depression — *the spleen.* By 1723, there were many circumstances which may well have reduced her to despair. All hope of ever marrying Swift—himself in bad health—must have vanished. Not Marriage but Death was now *in prospect.*

The years of frantic efforts to rescue her estate from the lawyers' clutches, *to get it into her own hands,* as Swift had written so long ago, had proved utterly fruitless. She no longer had the health or the hope necessary to struggle on. Indeed, Vanessa can scarcely be blamed if, as Dr. Delany alleges, she had tried to drown her misery by turning to Bacchus for comfort. It may be that with everything in tragic disorder, one thing remained which now urgently demanded settlement—a boy, aged about eight, who was boarded with a Dublin family named M'Loghlin. Before her death some provision must be made for his future—for Swift's son.

Although the two women had never met, it is reasonable to believe that, in the course of sixteen years, through conversations with Swift, a very clear picture of Stella must have been gradually formed in Vanessa's mind—this good, kindly, intelligent woman, the faithful friend of Swift's youth, who had a sister's devotion to him. Quite certainly, no other description of Stella can ever have been offered to Vanessa by Swift. He would have told her, as he told posterity, that *no scandal, censure or detraction ever came out of her mouth*, and also that *the follies of her own sex, she was inclined to extenuate, or to pity.*

Little wonder, then, if in her final despair, Vanessa's thoughts should turn to this benevolent, middle-aged friend of the Dean's, who, in her charity would *extenuate and pity* Vanessa's misfortunes, and, because of her sisterly devotion to Swift, be willing to give Swift's son that security which his mother had never been able to provide. There lay Vanessa's only hope, since, for a multitude of reasons, it was clearly impossible that Swift should take open responsibility for the boy.

And so, one day late in April, 1723, Vanessa — who would be dead in five weeks—wrote a letter to Stella. Remembering the passionate fervour which burns in so many of her letters, it is not difficult to imagine the eloquence with which she made her plea and the picture she drew of her intimate relations over sixteen years with Swift; her marriage-engagement; her life with him in London; her hopes and fears; the birth of the child; her relations with Swift since her return to Ireland. Secure in her absolute certainty of Stella's sisterly relationship with Swift, Vanessa would have anticipated nothing worse than a preliminary shock and surprise at Swift's weakness, followed immediately by Stella's loving *extenuation and pity.* When she had written her letter, Vanessa, worn out with emotion, must have felt certain that her appeal could not fail to touch Stella's warm heart and secure the child's future.

There is abundant testimony from her friends that Stella was, in every respect, a most admirable person. Even Dr. Evans, Bishop of Meath and Swift's bitter enemy, describes her as *a very good woman,* and Lord Orrery, who wastes little praise, is lyrical about her prefections. Swift, on the night of her death, described her as *the truest, most virtuous and valuable friend that I, or perhaps any other person, was ever blessed with.* He also stated that *when she was once convinced, by open facts, of any breach of Truth or Honour, in any person of high station, especially in the Church, she could not conceal her indignation.* He adds, *Honour, Truth, Liberality, Good-nature and Modesty were the virtues she chiefly possessed, and most valued in her acquaintance.*

Stella had been in love with Swift from her girlhood and had certainly suffered considerably because of his failure to marry her. Nevertheless, she had accepted his will and, but for periods of jealous misery, had contented herself with a highly privileged friendship.

She was, however, capable of jealousy and, about this time, wrote these lines:

On Jealousy

Oh! shield me from his rage, Celestial Powers!
This Tyrant that embitters all my hours.
Oh! Love, you've poorly played the Monarch's part,
You conquered, but you can't defend my heart;
So blessed was I throughout thy happy Reign,
I thought this Monster banish'd from thy Train;
But you would raise him to support thy Throne,

And now he claims your Empire as his own;
Or tell me, Tyrants, have you both agreed
That where One reigns, the Other shall succeed?

One version of the letter episode relates that, when Stella had read Vanessa's letter, she sent it to the Dean and, without giving time for an answer, fled from Dublin to hide herself in the country. Vanessa's letter, written in her absolute confidence that Stella had never been anything more than Swift's sisterly friend, would have carried a terrible conviction to the stricken woman. For Swift, no appeal was possible.

Most stories agree that he rode to Celbridge, threw Vanessa's letter before her and, after a terrible interview, stormed away, leaving Vanessa half-conscious. She had brought upon Swift the most dreaded of all eventualities: Stella, lover of Truth and Honour, had seen him in his naked shame.

It is easy to imagine the torrent of foul invectives that tore away the last shreds of Vanessa's endurance — Swift's appalling weapon, which he himself once described, in an apology to Stella,

And when indecently I rave,
When all my brutish passions break
With gall in every word I speak—

After the storm of rage and obscenity had passed over her, there was nothing—nothing but the terrible echoes of those *killing, killing words*. Later would come the feeble struggle to cleanse herself of the filth in which he had drowned her . . to rescue the long years he had distorted and defiled . . . to defend herself (above all, perhaps in Stella's eyes) from the horrible charges . . . She had not been his harlot . . . foisting her bastard . . . she was his affianced wife . . . She was . . . she *had* been . . . *the one person on earth he had loved, honoured, esteemed and adored* . . .

There was so little time . . . A day or two later, she made a new will. By then, the pain was numbed; her mind was clear again. She left the bulk of her considerable property to two strangers: to the Reverend George Berkeley, Fellow of Trinity College, whom she knew to be a good and upright man, on whose honesty and good faith she could rely to defend her good name, and to Robert Marshall a law student, whom she could summon to her bedside for her instructions about the publication of her papers. Between these two grateful men, she could be sure that the truth would be made clear. To the Archbishop of Dublin, her father's friend and her own, she left £25 for a mourning ring and the same bequest to the Archbishop of Clonfert. Swift had been on good terms with neither. They would be on *her* side. The first person named in her will, *Erasmus Lewis of London, Esq.* had known the truth from the beginning, when he used to forward her letters, under his cover, to Swift. She left a legacy to Dr. Bryan Robinson, one of Dublin's leading physicians, who had probably attended both Vanessa and her sister. A bequest to her faithful servant, Anne Kindon[1], who had come with her from London, where she had been Mrs. Van Homrigh's servant. Anne Kindon knew the truth too. Half a dozen other small bequests. *In witness thereof I, the said Esther Van Homrigh, have hereunto set my hand and seal, this first day of May, in the year of Our Lord* 1723.

The lawyer folded his papers and went away, tiptoeing, perhaps, as people tend to do in a sickroom. Outside, Turnstile Alley was very quiet.

She had made no provision in her will for the child. She could not, without naming—and branding—him. She could

---

[1]Anne Kindon witnessed an I.O.U. which Vanessa gave to one of her mother's creditors, in February 1713-14 (Monck Berkeley, *Literary Relics*).

only hope and trust in the ultimate goodness of the woman who had, unwittingly, brought this final catastrophe upon her. She had no other living soul to turn to . . . She was too tired to struggle any more.

A few weeks later, Vanessa was dead.

The Archbishop of Dublin must have been extremely perturbed to hear from the Reverend Dr. Sheridan that Mrs. Van Homrigh, recently dead, had left her executors instructions to publish letters which had passed between herself and the Dean of St. Patrick's. The Archbishop was no friend of the Dean, but he was concerned, very naturally, about the good name of the Church; and when the very agitated Dr. Sheridan told him that the papers were actually in the printers' hands, things must have looked most alarming. To increase the awkwardness of the situation, it seemed that the Dean had vanished from Dublin the day of Esther Van Homrigh's death, and Dr. Sheridan assured the Archbishop that neither his clergy nor his friends had the least idea where he had gone, and were, therefore, unable to make any contact. Meanwhile, Mr. Marshall had taken his dying benefactress' wishes very seriously indeed, and all appeals from the Dean's clerical friends had failed to induce him to stop publication. Hence, Dr. Sheridan's despairing visit to the Archbishop — the last person to whom Swift's friends would have wished to admit the Dean's dilemma. By his flight, Swift had left them powerless. His behaviour in this emergency was exactly described in his own words:

Nothing more unqualifies a man to act with prudence than a misfortune that is attended with shame and guilt.

With complete lack of all prudence, he ran away. It is to be hoped that *shame and guilt* were aggravated by sorrow—sorrow for the dead woman whom he had loved for so many years, and for the living woman whom he had also grossly betrayed.

To the Archbishop, the danger of scandal would have been paramount—scandal which he may well have feared would prove only too well-grounded. As friend of both Esther Van Homrigh and of her father, he was well placed to advise young Robert Marshall as to his proper course. There were other powerful pressures which could be brought to bear on a law student, not yet called to the Bar, with his career to consider. A word here, a word there could make him realise the strength of the power he was challenging. Young Mr. Marshall was eventually induced to have second thoughts.

As Dr. Evans, Bishop of Meath reported, a few weeks later to the Archbishop of Canterbury,

> *The Archbishop of Dublin and the whole Irish posse have (I fear) prevailed with Mr. Marshall not to print the papers etc. as she desired, lest one of their own dear joyes should be trampled over by the Philistines.*

So, young Mr. Marshall was *prevailed* upon to remove the letters and papers from the printer's press; but he resolutely resisted suggestions that they should be destroyed. Some copies of the poem *Cadenus and Vanessa* rather mysteriously got into circulation, giving gossip plenty of food and adding to Stella's misery. But that was the only item of Vanessa's papers which reached the public for forty-four years. In 1767 the elderly Judge Robert Marshall, late of His Majesty's Court of Common Pleas, gave a small selection of the *Vanessa-Swift Correspondence* for publication. In 1921, all the surviving papers were published, for the first time, almost two centuries after Vanessa's death.

It is quite obvious from Vanessa's own numbering of the letters that many have been removed from the file. And not a single one has survived that was written during the last nine months of her life. Who did the censoring will never be known. Dr. Berkeley was far too occupied with his Bermuda scheme to have spared much time for such trifles. If, as seems likely, Mr. Marshall decided which letters should survive, he probably removed those which too obviously proved the existence of a child.

X

IN October 1723, five months after Vanessa's death, a reconciliation had taken place between Stella and Dean Swift, and the Ladies were back in their lodgings, *Near Liffey's stinking tide in Dublin,* to quote the verses with which he celebrated their return. Possibly, he may still have dreaded the ordeal that the ailing Stella would have to face in Dublin—and the impetus her return might give to the scandalmongers—because, about this time, he gave a money-order for £100 to Rebecca Dingley. Perhaps he hoped that, with the money, the Ladies might be persuaded to pay the expenses of a visit to their native land, possibly to one of the Spas to which they were so addicted. Swift was not the man to part lightly with so large a sum of money. But Mrs. Dingley never made any use of the £100, nor did she return it to Swift, but disposed of it, in her will, many years later—one of the very minor mysteries of the story.

But Stella did return to Dublin. Scandal died away, and the *obloquy* from which Swift had fled had spent the force of its first venom. A very solid phalanx had formed to protect the Dean's reputation, both from the truth, and also from the lies of popular report. His friends had assiduously spread the story that the innocent, luckless Dean had been the victim of an hysterical young woman's unruly passion; that only his kindness of heart had prevented him from dealing with her as ruthlessly as she deserved; that he was a blameless, much maligned man, meriting nothing but sympathy. Those who had heard more or less detailed reports about the letters—which, after all, had been seen by printers and very likely discussed by young Mr. Marshall, before he was *prevailed* upon to forget them—were assured, on no less high an authority than that of the Reverend Doctor Delany, that *his letters contain nothing but curt compliments, excuses, apologies and thanks for little presents . . . but not the least hint of criminal commerce between them, in the letters of either.*

The conspiracy of silence was complete amongst those who knew the *whole* truth; Stella, Swift and probably the Reverend Dr. Sheridan, loving friend of both and later an executor of Stella's will. To their number must be added whoever censored the Correspondence. The Archbishop and his clergy were silent because they had to protect the Church from scandal. Swift's enemies, amongst whom the Bishop of Meath and Dean Smedley ranked prominently, threw what stones local rumours made available to their hands, with unseemly enthusiasm. But the staunch friends of Stella and of the Dean stood firm and protected his reputation against all attacks.

There was nobody to protect Vanessa's good name, her executors having been *prevailed upon* to retire, and the most sympathetic picture of her is that of a young woman *who loved the reluctant Dean greatly but extremely unwisely.* Nevertheless, in *one* hope the luckless Vanessa may not have failed, trusting as she did in the basic goodness of Stella.

There have always been rumours that a boy existed, who was a son of Swift and Stella. Such stories were told during their lifetimes.

When Monck Berkeley, grandson of Vanessa's heir, came to Dublin about 1788, he found Richard Brennan, then an elderly man, a member of the staff of St. Patrick's Cathedral. He had been Dean Swift's last servant, and had protected the old man on the occasion of his alarming experience with the Reverend Dr. Wilson. This is the account of Brennan, published in Monck Berkeley's *Literary Relics*:

My informant was Richard Brennan, at present a bell-ringer in St. Patrick's, and in a state of penury. (Such should not be the case—the servant in whose arms Swift breathed his last, and who attended him during the six years immediately preceding his death.) My informer, who is still living in Dublin, told me that, when he was a boy at school, there was a boy boarded with the Master, who was commonly reputed to be the Dean's son by Mrs. Johnson. He added that the boy strongly resembled the Dean in his complexion; that he dined constantly at the Deanery on Sunday, and that, when the other boys were driven out of the Deanery yard, he was suffered to remain there and divert himself. This boy survived Mrs. Johnson by a year or two at the most.

If Robert Brennan had been about the same age as this schoolmate, he would have been about seventy-four when Monck Berkeley interviewed him in Dublin in 1788; about twenty-five when he went to the Deanery as Swift's last man-servant, and about nine in 1723 when Vanessa died. There is no reason to discount the accuracy of Brennan's school memories, nor to doubt that rumours of this mysterious child —*little master*?—were in circulation in Dublin soon after Vanessa's death. Monck Berkeley was sufficiently impressed with Brennan's bona fides to give him a pension.

The reference to the boys playing in the Deanery yard would seem to point to the school of St. Patrick's Cathedral as being the one at which the child was a boarder. There is no explanation of how this reputed son of Stella and Swift got there unless, indeed, Vanessa's last desperate appeal bore fruit when Stella returned to Dublin, after recovering from her shock and heartbreak. From everything that is known of that remarkable woman, with her love of truth and justice, it is extremely likely that on her return to Dublin she would have lost little time in finding the child—this boy who so *resembled the Dean*. With or without Swift's immediate consent, she would have insisted on this child's right to proper schooling and care. The moral courage of this woman—whose physical courage had been sufficient for her to shoot dead a man who was breaking into her lodgings—would not have been daunted by the fear of provoking further scandal, where the child's future was at stake. But, during the few years she had still to live, when ill-natured rumours buzzed, Stella must often have been bitterly hurt and sorely tempted to defend her innocence with the truth. About this time, Swift wrote some lines, *On Censure,* which may very well have been written to encourage her, ending, as they do, with the suggestion that she ignore gossip, since *ten hundred thousand lyes* cannot make her *less virtuous, learn'd or wise.*

Bare innocence is no support
When you are tried in scandal's court . . .
The world, a willing stander-by,
Inclines to aid the specious lye;
Alas, they would not do you wrong,
But all appearances are strong.
Yet whence proceeds this weight we lay
On what detracting people say?
For let mankind discharge their tongues
In venom, till they burst their lungs,
Their utmost malice cannot make
Your head, or tooth, or finger ake:
Nor spoil your shape, distort your face
Or put one feature out of place.
Nor will you find your fortune sink
By what they speak, or what they think;
Nor can ten hundred thousand lyes
Make you less virtuous, learn'd or wise.
The most effectual way to baulk
Their malice is . . . to let them talk

From the Dean's point of view, any amount of *talk* was better than a declaration that the child's real mother was

Vanessa. Such an avowal might have saved Stella's reputation, but would certainly have given new life to the old scandals about his relationship with the dead woman. That, he could or would not face.

Nevertheless, Stella's consciousness of her false position may well explain the curious story of a half-overheard conversation between herself and the Dean, during her last illness. He is reported to have said,

Well, my dear, if you wish it, it shall be owned.

To which Stella answered, with a sigh,

It is too late.

This is usually explained as Swift's last-moment offer to admit a secret marriage; but it is more likely that the Dean, tormented by sorrow at the sight of her sufferings, was at last offering to clear her reputation from the stigma of being the mother of the child who was then living with her, *on charity.*

Unfortunately for this child, Stella had only a few years left in which to supervise his life and, during her last years, she was often at death's door. Hence, perhaps, his period at a boarding school.

In 1727, she made a will, a few weeks before her death. Being the prudent, orderly woman she was, and remembering her constant illnesses over years, it is difficult to believe that she had never made a previous will, so that the one she made in December 1727 may have a special significance. For the last months of her life, she had been living near the Phoenix Park, in the hope, perhaps, that the good country air might ease the tortures of asthma. She described herself as *being in tolerable health in body and perfectly sound mind* and she bequeathed the bulk of her small fortune to her mother and sister for their lives, and afterwards to Steevens Hospital, Dublin, for the support of a Chaplain.

She also gave instructions that, should the Church of Ireland ever be dis-established, her money should immediately revert to her nearest living relative. The Church of Ireland was dis-established in 1871, and her sister, Mrs. Filby, had no less than nineteen children.

Stella left several other legacies, amongst them one which seems to have remained unnoticed:

> *I bequeath to Bryan M'Loghlin (a child who now lives with me and whom I keep on charity) twenty-five pounds, to bind him out apprentice, as my executors and the survivors of them shall think fit.*

In 1727, £25 was a fairly considerable sum of money; in that year, the fee paid to apprentice a boy, by the parish school of St. Nicholas Without, Dublin, was £3 *and a suit of clothes.* Over and above this legacy, Swift has recorded that, in her strong-box, which she bequeathed to him, there was about £150 in gold. Perhaps this money, too, was intended to provide indirectly for the child, as the relatively wealthy Dean had no particular need for it. During the three years that Stella had given a home to Bryan M'Loghlin, the childless woman may well have become very attached to the boy and much concerned about his future. That Bryan was an affectionately established member of Stella's household is curiously corroborated by Dean Swift himself.

Rebecca Dingley had all her life been a dog-worshipper, and when her adored Tiger died, Swift wrote a cruelly jocose verse on her loss The introduction runs as follows:

Elegy upon Tiger
Her dear Lady's joy and comfort
Who departed this Life
The last day of March 1727,
To the great joy of Bryan
That his antagonist is gone.

Tiger, surprisingly, was a female, as Swift adds this note:

N. B. *She died in Puppy and left two helpless infants behind. And that Mrs. Sally and Jane and Robin cryed three days for.*

The pampered lap-dog may well have been less popular with the twelve year old Bryan! Presumably Mrs. Sally, Jane and Robin were the *two maids and one man* to whom Swift alludes later in his description of Stella's household. In March 1727, that household was nearing its end, since Stella spent the last months of her life with friends, where she died nine months later.

Amongst Stella's executors, who were to decide Bryan's future was one of her oldest and most devoted friends, whom she could trust to obey her wishes, the Rev. Dr. Sheridan. He constantly attended her during her last illness, and would have done his utmost to carry out any instructions she gave. He and Swift had a serious quarrel immediately after Stella's death, and it was a long time, according to his son, before they made friends again. It is reasonable to believe that Stella's death produced yet another crisis about the child's future, and that Swift and Sheridan disagreed violently.

There is another signficant feature of this will, made by a dying woman a few weeks before her death—the detailed description of the boy's status. It is as if in her last public declaration, Stella were determined to silence the malicious rumours, which had so embittered her final years. Bryan M'Loghlin had no other claim upon her than her *charity*.

And the name, M'Loghlin? Kendall, who provided facilities for the weekly meetings of Vanessa and the Dean must, undoubtedly, have been a person whom they both knew to be utterly trustworthy. Kendall married a woman named M'Loghlin, and it is a reasonable surmise that

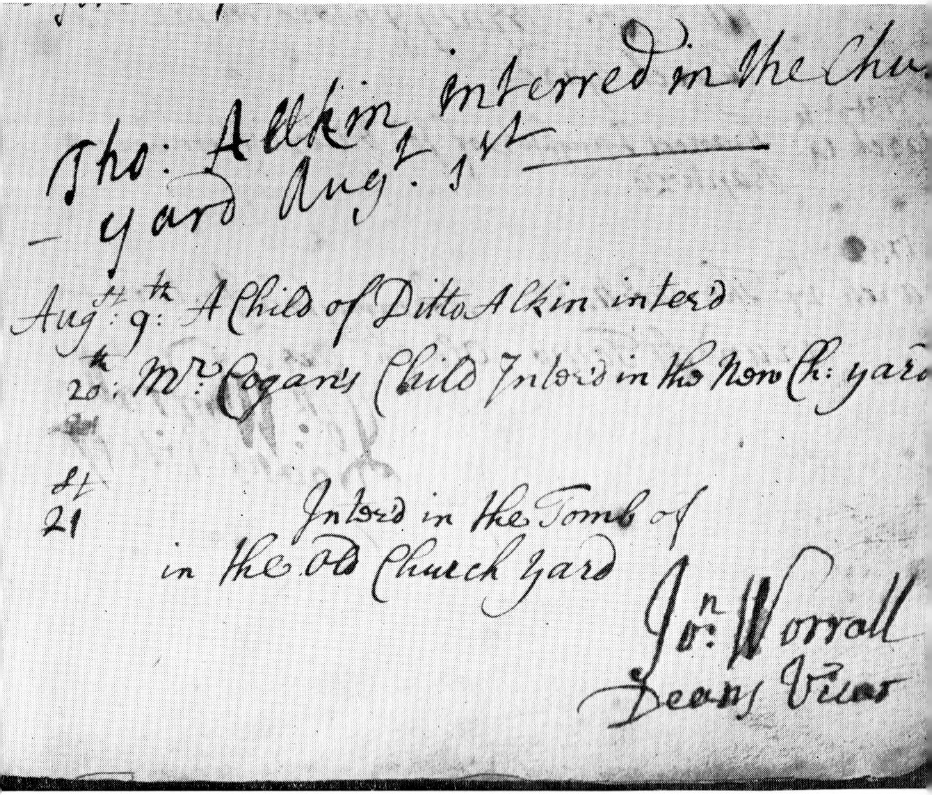

Tho: Allkin interred in the Chu
— yard Augt. 1st

Augst: 9th: A Child of Ditto Alkin inter'd
20th: Mr: Cogan's Child Inter'd in the New Ch: yar
21 Inter'd in the Tomb of
in the Old Church yard

Jon: Worrall
Deans Vicar

PLATE II

The anonymous burial entry in the Register of Saint Patrick's Cathedral Dublin.

Vanessa boarded her son with this family and that they lent this nameless child their own name.

According to Richard Brennan, the boy *survived Mrs. Johnson a year or two at most.* Stella died at the beginning of 1728. Some two and a half years later, there appears a very curious entry of a burial in the Register of St. Patrick's Cathedral,

> 21*st August*, 1731.
> *inter'd in the tomb of*
> *in the old Churchyard.*

Immediately beneath this entry is the signature of the Rev. John Worrall, who was Swift's Dean's Vicar and his trusted man of business. Apparently Mr. Worrall was content to sign this extraordinary registration, although no similar one exists in the Records of St. Patrick's Cathedral: an unidentified corpse, interred in some unidentified owner's unidentified tomb. It is also significant that this should have taken place in the only cemetery where such a burial could be arranged, without any awkward questioning, and that the date was within *a year or two* of Stella's death, as Brennan had reported.

The mystery surrounding this extraordinary interment is very unlikely to be cleared away, but a possible solution would point to this nameless tomb as the last resting place of *little Master*, of the anonymous schoolboy who so resembled the Dean, of little Bryan M'Loghlin, who lived with Stella and was jealous of the lap-dog—of the ill-fated son of Esther Van Homrigh and Jonathan Swift, Dean of St. Patrick's Dublin.

*

Swift survived, for many years, both the women who loved him. During that time, he wrote a collection of verses on women and *Love,* so grossly appalling that, to quote Carl Van Doren, *they made even the Eighteenth Century squirm.* That was not a squeamish period, yet Letitia Pilkington records in her Memoirs that her mother vomited when first she read *The Lady's Dressing-room.* It is as if some demon drove a lapsed lover to desecrate, with obscene scrawlings, the shrine at which he had once worshipped.

A persistent legend relates that, when his terrible years ended at last in the Winter of 1745, amongst his papers was found an envelope, on which he had written: *Only a woman's hair.* Inside was a brown tress. Stella's hair, as Swift has recorded, was *black as a crow.*

APPENDICES & BIBLIOGRAPHY

Appendix I: The Paternity of Thomas, Jane and Jonathan Swift

In the Burial Register of the Church of St. Andrew, Northborough, Northamptonshire, the following entry is to be found for the date, 3rd December, 1737.

Thos. Swift, Bro. to Dr. Jon. Swift, Dean of St. Patrick's, Dublin.

This very remarkable entry is, according to the present Rector, the Reverend A. Lister, *in writing similar to several previous entries.* There is no doubt that Thomas Swift was buried in the churchyard of St. Andrew, on 3rd December 1737 as brother of Dean Swift.

Mr. P. I. King, M. A. Archivist at the Northamptonshire Record Office has kindly supplied the information that the clergyman then in charge of St. Andrew's was the Reverend William Richardson, Rector of the nearby Parish of Elton from 1717 to 1741. He took his B.A. at St. John's College, Cambridge in 1696 when he was twenty-two; so that, at the time of Thomas Swift's burial, Mr. Richardson would have been about sixty-four and have been in charge of the parish for over twenty years. The entry and identification could not have been made without his knowledge and, presumably, approval. But the contemporary transcripts of the St. Andrew Register, which are deposited in the Northamptonshire Archives, do *not* contain this entry.

As Mr. King explains, . . . *every year, at the Archdeacon's Visitation of the Parishes, the Rector hands him a copy of the entries in his Register, for the previous year.* Mr. King confirms that this entry has been omitted from the copy of the 1737 Register, given to the Archdeacon. This omission is, in itself, very curious. It would seem that it was one thing to acknowledge Thomas Swift's identity in a small community, where his background was probably well known, but quite another to announce, to the wider world outside, that the dead man was brother of the famous, still living, Dean of St. Patrick's.

Regarding the wording of the burial entry, Mr. King says, *it is* not *usual to give details of relationships in 18th century burial registers, except that children have their parents' names given. I should think it very rare to mention that somebody was a brother.*

Mr. King also gives the information that there *were Swifts residing in the Northborough and neighbouring parishes.* There were also Temples living at Sulby, some thirty miles from Northborough. Any wills or documents relating to local Swifts would seem to show that they were humble folk, shepherds and such like; lowly connections, possibly, of the Swifts of Dublin, amongst whom it would be convenient to find suitable foster-parents for a boy of that name, whose birth followed a marriage too soon for comfort.

This marriage, for which the Archbishop of Armagh issued a Special Licence, in June 1664, was that of Jonathan Swift and *Abigail Erick, of the City of Dublin, Spinster.* The advantage of this expensive form of marriage licence is that the ceremony is performed in private and therefore no date need be registered.

The bride, an Englishwoman from Leicestershire, was some ten years older than her bridegroom, and was given an annuity of £20, in English Funds, ostensibly by her husband, who possessed no apparent means.

Denis Johnston, in his book, *In search of Swift*, has put up a well-reasoned argument that Sir John Temple, Master of the Rolls in Dublin, was the father of Jonathan Swift, the last child of this marriage. It would seem that his contention would be enormously strengthened by arguing that

Sir John was the father of *all* Abigail Erick's children, and that Thomas, born probably about the Winter of 1664, was the eldest.

In that case, the procedure after birth, with both sons would have been the same; Thomas was removed to England because he was born *too soon* after the marriage by which Swift gave Abigail Erick the protection of his name, while Jonathan was removed to England because he was born *too late* after the death of his putative father.

Between these two sons, there was born a daughter, Jane, baptised in St. Michan's Church, Dublin, in May 1666, almost two years after the marriage. She spent the greater part of her youth in Dublin, and will be considered later.

Soon after Jonathan Swift's birth, he was removed from Dublin. The story is that he was kidnapped by an over-affectionate nurse, who had to go to England, and could not bear to leave the infant behind her. This episode Swift himself characterises as *very unusuell*, which it certainly was; but not more so than the subsequent events. The infant remained in this woman's keeping by the direction of the mother, who feared a sea-journey for the child, but had no fear of leaving him in charge of the woman who had criminally removed him from his mother's Dublin home. Odder still, Mrs. Swift returned to her native Leicestershire, after some years, making her permanent home there and living frugally on her £20 annuity. As Denis Johnson points out, it would seem natural that she would then have taken immediate steps to be reunited with the child she had not seen for some years. But it would appear that this was not so; the infant Jonathan was, according to Hawkesworth, *again carried to Ireland by his nurse and replaced under the protection of his Uncle Godwin.*

Had poverty been the reason that Mrs. Swift relinquished her child to her brother-in-law, it is obvious that a very small part of the money which was henceforth spent on the young boy would have supported him comfortably in his mother's care. Why, then, was *this* child brought back to Dublin?

Swift himself tells that he was an infant prodigy; by the time the erring nurse brought him back to Ireland he could spell and read any chapter of the Bible. Although neither Swift himself nor other authorities agree as to his exact age at this time—the highest estimate is five—there is no doubt that the small boy already showed very great promise round about the year 1671.

By one of those odd coincidences which sometimes make truth far stranger than fiction, in that same year, Sir Philip Skippon of Wrentham, Suffolk, wrote to his friend, Mr. John Ray, on 18th September, 1671,

> *I shall somewhat surprise you with what I have seen in a little boy, William Wooton, five years old last month, son of Mr. Wooton, Minister of this Parish, who hath instructed his child, within the last three quarters of a year, in the reading of the Latin, Greek and Hebrew languages, which he can read almost as well as English, and that tongue he could read at four years and four months old, almost as well as lads thrice his age.*

This William Wooton, infant prodigy, so nearly Swift's exact contemporary, became in due course a close friend of Bentley and, with him, disputed with Sir William Temple in the controversy about Ancient and Modern Learning. Later Wooton was a severe critic of Swift's *Tale of a Tub*, and was a victim of Swift's wit.

It was the age of the Infant Prodigy in England. John Evelyn's son had died, some years before, already famous at five. At two and a half, his father records that he could read perfectly *any of the English, Latin, French or Gothic letters, pronouncing the three first languages exactly.* His accomplishments at the time of his death, aged five, were too long to list here.

Evelyn's child had obviously had every possible assistance and encouragement in acquiring his terrifying load of learning, while the baby Jonathan, presumably, had only whatever poor facilities were available in his foster-mother's humble circle.

Sir John Temple, Master of the Rolls in Dublin, was himself a man of learning. His father had been Provost of Trinity College, Dublin. Sir John had been a Scholar of that College, became a B.A. when he was under eighteen and an M.A. in 1620. In the same year, he was admitted to Lincoln's Inn. If it had been reported to him that this nurse-child in England were showing promise of very remarkable intelligence he might well have decided to make an entirely new arrangement for his future, which would give this infant prodigy opportunities for an education worthy of his talents. The boy's return to Dublin provided this fully and the presence of the Swift brothers made arrangements very easy for Sir John. They were reasonably prosperous lawyers more than willing to oblige the powerful Master of the Rolls. Henceforth, a great deal of money was spent on Jonathan Swift's education, for which he never showed the slightest gratitude, which is all the more remarkable since very few of the Swifts' own sons had any comparable opportunities. There has never been any satisfactory explanation offered as to why this destitute child should have been singled out for a far more expensive education than should have been his normal lot.

Sir John Temple lived on in Dublin, until his death in 1677, and must have taken a keen interest in the progress of this unusual child; his will was never published, and as it is now destroyed, it is impossible to know what, if any, arrangements he made for his family; but his son John

Temple continued in Dublin and was in a position to see that his father's wishes were carried out.

There is no open avowal of any Temple interest whatever in Mrs. Abigail Swift's children, until 1689, when Deane Swift, reporting an imaginary recommendation which she gave to Jonathan, whom she was sending to Sir William Temple for a start in life, makes her say,

> *. . . his father, Sir John Temple, had a regard and friendship for your father and your uncles until his last hour.*

Swift, in his Autobiography, referring to Sir William Temple, states,

> *. . . his father had been a great friend to the family.*

How that great friendship manifested itself is not explained by either Deane Swift or the Dean of St. Patrick's.

However, from 1689 onwards, the Temple family became open patrons of Jane and Jonathan Swift, and remained in this role for very many years. He spent a considerable time as a member of Sir William's household; his sister paid lengthy visits there.

Jane Swift, (born about April 1666, some two years after the marriage of Abigail Erick), is described by Deane Swift as *rather beyond what is called agreeable*, meaning, presumably, that she was rather a pleasant girl. According to F. Elrington Ball, she was married from the house of William Swift, and it would appear that, during her early life, she was probably a member of his household. Little is known about William Swift, except dates, but there is evidence that he was a kindly man. He was very helpful to Abigail Swift after her husband's death, aiding her to clear up the muddle in which he had left his legal accounts; he was on good terms with Jonathan, who seems to have felt kindly towards him. When Swift's mother finally left Dublin for her native Leicestershire, she must presumably have been content with an arrangement by which her baby daughter was left behind in someone's keeping. It may well have been in William Swift's family.

He came to Dublin, from England, in 1661, bringing a new wife. In Dublin, he was admitted an attorney. He married four times, he fathered and lost a number of children. At the outbreak of the Williamite Wars, his family shared the flight to England of the frightened Anglo-Irish community. Presumably, young Jane went with them, and later returned with her guardian's family, to Dublin, where life soon became normal again.

Jane Swift certainly spent long periods at Moor Park and at the London home of the Temple family. In a letter to William Swift, her brother Jonathan wrote:

Moor Park, November 29, 1692.

Sir,

My sister told me you was pleased (when she was here) to wonder I did so seldom write to you . . . I knew your aversion to impertinence; and God knows so very private a life as mine can furnish a letter with little else; for I often am two or three months without seeing anybody besides the family; and now that my sister is gone, I am likely to be more solitary than before.

This letter also contains about the only tribute ever paid by Swift to his relations,

I am sorry my fortune should fling me far from the best of my relations, but I hope I shall have the happiness to see you some time or other.

There is a letter to Jane, in a collection of Swift's letters, edited by Deane Swift and published in Dublin by Faulkner in 1768. Deane Swift heads the letter, *Dr. Swift to Mrs. Jane Swift* and adds a note, *The Doctor's sister.* It is dated 1696 and is obviously written from Moor Park to a member of the Temple household then in residence in Sir

William's house in London. As Lady Temple (who had made her home there for many years before her death) had died in London not very long previously, her sister-in-law Lady Giffard (who all that time had been head of Sir William's establishment in Moor Park) may well have been making a prolonged stay in the Pall Mall house.

For some reason this letter has been *re-addressed* to Stella or to her mother, Mrs. Bridget Johnson, by some subsequent editors, the reason perhaps, being that they could not imagine Swift writing a humorously affectionate letter to anyone else. Here is the letter to Jane Swift.

1696.

I received your kind letter from Robert, by word of mouth, and think it a vast condescention in you to think of us in your greatness; now shall we hear nothing from you for five months but We courtiers. *Loory is well, and presents his humble duty to my Lady, and love to his fellow servant: but he is the miserablest creature in the world; eternally in his melancholy note, whatever I can do; and if his finger do but ake, I am in such a fright you would wonder at it. I pray return my service to Mrs. Filby in payment of hers by Robert.*

Nothing grows better by your absence but my Lady's chamber-floor, and Tumble-down Dick. Here are three letters for you, and Molly will not send one of them; she says you ordered her to the contrary. Mr. Mose and I desire you will remember our love to the King, and let us know how he looks.

Robert says the Czar is there, and is fallen in love with you, and designs to carry you to Muscovy, pray provide yourself with muffs and sable tippets etc.

Aeolus has made a strange revolution in the rook's nests; but I say no more, for it is dangerous to meddle with things above us.

I desire your absence heartily; for now I live in great state, and the cook comes in to know what I please to have for dinner; I ask, very gravely, what is in the house, and accordingly give orders for a dish of pigeons, or etc. You shall have no more ale here; unless you send us a letter. Here is a great bundle, and a letter for you; both came together from London. We all keep home like so many cats.

Regarding the date, the allusion to Peter the Great's visit to England would seem to show that 1696 should read 1698, since that was the year in which the Czar used to amuse himself by being pushed in a wheel-barrow through John Evelyn's magnificent beech hedges, as the owner indignantly records. On the other hand, the entire letter is written in a jocose humour, and rumours of the Czar's impending visit may have long anticipated the event. The account of the health and behaviour of Lady Giffard's adored *Loory* might have helped to place the letter, had her brother, Sir William, dated the poem he wrote for her, on the death of that much lamented bird—

> ... *and now, alas, embalmed with her tears* ...
> ... *Company, Love, Playfellow and Friend* ...

The importance of this letter is that it shows that Jane is again spending many months as a member of the Temple household. It also shows, by its atmosphere of easy affection, that the *disagreement that subsisted between* the brother and sister, according to Deane Swift, had not yet arisen.

But the days of the Temple household at Moor Park were rapidly drawing to a close. In May, 1699, Sir William Temple died, and that hospitable home was broken up.

It may have been no coincidence that six months later Jane married Joseph Fenton. The marriage was bitterly opposed by her brother, who, according to Deane Swift, offered her £500 if she would break it off. While it seems extremely unlikely that Swift had so large a sum to dispose of, the story at least proves the strength of his objections. Nevertheless, Jane married Fenton and, from some unexplained source, was provided with a comfortable dowry of £300.

The marriage was unhappy, and some ten or eleven years later she left her husband, a perilous step for an ostensibly penniless gentlewoman, with at least two children, who had no other home to go to in Dublin, her kind guardian, William Swift, having died six years earlier.

In May, 1710, Jonathan Swift made this entry,

On Wednesday, between seven and eight in the evening, I received a letter in my chamber at Laracor from Mrs. Fenton, dated 9th May, with one enclosed sent from Mrs. Worrall at Leicester to Mrs. Fenton, giving an account that my mother, Mrs. Abigail Swift, died that morning, Monday, April 24th, 1710, *about ten o'clock after a long illness; being ill all winter and lame and extremely ill a month or six weeks before her death. I have now lost my barrier between myself and death. God grant I may live to be as well prepared for it as I confidently believe her to have been. If the way to Heaven be through piety, justice and charity, she is there.*

In January, 1710-11, Swift explains in his *Journal to Stella* that,

Mrs. Fenton has written me another letter about some money of hers, in Lady Giffard's hands, that is entrusted to me by my mother, not to come to her husband.

Mrs. Fenton was still, apparently, in Dublin, and Lady Giffard was handling some money belonging to Jane, which she was anxious her husband should know nothing about. Within a matter of months, Mrs. Fenton had joined Lady

Giffard's establishment in England, where, in company with Stella's mother, she remained until old Lady Giffard's death in 1722, broke up yet another Temple shelter.

But, to return to 1711, there is a curious entry in the Journal, dated 17th July,

It is damned news you tell me about Mrs. F., it makes me love England less a great deal. I know nothing of the trunk being left or taken; so 'tis odd enough if the things in it were mine; and I think I was told there were some things for me, that my mother left particularly for me.

Unfortunately, the trunk and its contents are not again referred to, so it is not possible to know what *papers* may have reached Swift from his dead mother or what family secrets he may then have learned. But it may well be of significance that, according to Deane Swift, the Doctor was *upon no Terms of Friendship* with any of the Swift family, nor they with him, after his return to Ireland from this London visit. Whatever tenuous ties held him to his relatives in Dublin were now broken, for very many years.

What his sister had said or done to make him *love England less a great deal* is not known, but the cause of his anger was not, apparently, her leaving her husband, as a few weeks later he writes,

I pity poor Jenny, but her husband is a dunce, and with respect to him she loses little by her deafness.

In the same month, the Journal records that

Mrs. Fenton was to see me about a week ago; and desired I would get her son into the Charter House.

The relevance of these extracts appears only when they are contrasted with a letter, written by Dean Swift to Benjamin Motte, his English man of business, dated 25th October, 1735.

Dublin.

. . . Here lives one Mr. Hatch, who is a manager for the Temple family. He came lately to the Deanery, and talked with great melancholy of Mrs. Fenton not having received any money from me, for a long time; whereupon I paid him ten guineas and took his receipt; for, to say the truth, having not heard from you in a long time, nor caring one straw whether the woman had received one penny or what became of her, who, during her whole life, disobliged me in most circumstances by her conduct, I did not employ one thought upon her except to her disadvantage, and I heartily wish you had demanded your money of me, as you paid it, because then it would not have been such a load upon me as now it will . . . . I desire, therefore that you will pay her no more, but only send me how her account lies, including the ten guineas I sent by Mr. Hatch, who was to send her a bill . . . . I would much rather assist my poor cousin Lancelot, if it was in my power, for she was always kind and obliging to me. I did not know Mrs. Fenton had a son, nor will ever believe such a breed had either worth or honour —— ?

Some explanation of this letter is necessary. Mr. Hatch (who gave his name to a Dublin street) was, as Swift explains, the Irish agent of the Temple estates. It seems extremely unlikely that Mr. Hatch would have had the temerity—or the impertinence—to call upon Dean Swift to reproach him for not having paid Mrs. Fenton's allowance, if the payment of that allowance were not part of his business as the Temple family's agent. Swift's anger at the interview (at which he actually paid ten guineas to Mr. Hatch, on behalf of Mrs. Fenton) is quite apparent in this letter; had the annuity to his sister been a matter of his own private charity, there is little doubt of the reception Temple's agent would have got from the infuriated Dean. As it was, since Swift had had no account for a year from Motte, he had no option but to pay the money to the Temple's agent, on behalf of his sister. It would seem very clear that the money Mrs. Fenton received was Temple money, of which Swift was merely the channel; the fact that Mrs. Fenton (then living again near Moor Park in Surrey) should have applied to the Temple agent when her annuity was in arrears, is proof that she *knew* the money was Temple money.

A further proof that the payment to Mrs. Fenton was not a voluntary offering from the Dean is given by his allusion to his cousin, Mrs. Lancelot, whom he would much rather assist *if it were in my power, for she was always kind and obliging to me.* (This lady, formerly Mrs. Patty Rolt, had always been a favourite of Swift's; he sympathised with her poverty, in London, where she lived in the absence of her first husband. For some reason, various editors have surmised that he was a good-for-nothing, runaway spouse, although it seems obvious from an entry in the *Journal* (10th April, 1713) that he was a soldier in the English forces, stationed in Minorca. The Eighteenth Century Army provided no allowance for wives, and poor Mrs. Rolt had to live on £18 a year.) From the Dean's furious outburst against his sister, it seems extremely unlikely that he would have continued to support her, had he any option whatsoever. He goes so far, in his diatribe, as to deny any knowledge of Mrs. Fenton's son, whom he had been trying to get into the Charter House, some years before. It is satisfactory to see, in a letter from Mr. Motte to the Dean, that he considers *Mr. Fenton a man of worth and honour.*

When Lady Giffard died, in 1722, she left Mrs. Fenton some of her clothes, the furnishings of her bedroom, a small silver cup, and thirty guineas. After Lady Giffard's establishment was broken up, Jane Fenton went straight back to

Guilford in Surrey, to the neighbourhood of the Temples in Moor Park. The *silver cup* which Jane Fenton inherited from Lady Giffard is presumably the *silver cann,* which Mrs. Fenton left to *Anne, wife of Richard Fenton, son of my late husband, Joseph Fenton, by his first wife.*

Her will, dated February, 1733-4, and put into Probate in March, 1735-6, has also been overlooked. It is of interest for several reasons; it proves that Mrs. Fenton did *not* die in 1738, as stated by the Rev. Dr. Lyon and quoted by W. Monck Mason and others; it also proves that Joseph Fenton, at the time of his marriage to Jane Swift, was a widower with at least two children. By her marriage with Fenton, she also had at least two children: a son, to whom reference has already been made, and a daughter, who married Jonathan Jackson, who had a daughter, Jane.

Although the amount of her property is unspecified, it is obvious from her will that Mrs. Fenton was in comfortable circumstances and in no way dependent on the money which the Temples' agent, Mr. Hatch, was demanding from the Dean, a few months before her death. She leaves £10 to the poor, £2 to the clergyman who preached at her funeral, a few small bequests including one to Stella's mother, who had become Mrs. Mose by her second marriage, who is described as *now or late of Farnham.*

Incidentally, the will shows that Mrs. Fenton and Mrs. Mose were *not* living together in Farnham, as is usually stated. The legacy to Mrs. Swift is another tiny link with the Temples, whose Chaplain her husband had been.

But the real interest of the will is that it shows that Jane Fenton, whose husband had been a bankrupt, had sufficient property to set up a trust for the support and education of her granddaughter, Jane Jackson. Since Mrs. Fenton's only visible sources of income were a salary of £12 a year, during her service with Lady Giffard, and £20 from her brother, Dean Swift, it is difficult to see where the property came from which she disposed of in her will, unless it were the same mysterious source, which had provided her dowry, some thirty years earlier.

Jane Fenton died in Guilford on the 26th February, 1735-6, in the neighbourhood of Moor Park. She died, as she had lived, in the protecting shadow of the Temples.

With regard to Swift's possible knowledge of the paternity of his family, there are a few small clues remaining, which may help to strengthen conjectures. In a letter to Lord Bolingbroke, the Dean wrote,

Dublin, 31st October, 1729.

. . . . . *My birth, although from a family not undistinguished in its time, is many degrees inferior to yours. All my pretensions upon person and parts, infinitely so. I am a younger son of younger sons. You are born to a great fortune* . . . .

It must be remembered that Swift claimed his *mother's* family was one of great importance and antiquity. The phrase *I am a younger son* is, at least, unexpected from an *only* son.

Again, in No. VI of the *Drapier Letters,* he writes a name, which raises a query:

A gentleman, now in Dublin, affirms that, passing some months ago through Northampton . . . . . *that large town* . . . . *directly on our way to London* . . . .

Did the Dean of St. Patrick's learn — perhaps from his mother's delayed trunk — of the existence of Thomas Swift . . . . and did they ever meet?

In the MS. of the Rev. Dr. Lyon, Minor Canon of St. Patrick's during Swift's lifetime, he records that, in 1738, *the Dean put on mourning for his sister.* As is now known, Mrs. Fenton had then been dead for several years. But in December 1737, *Thos. Swift, Bro. to Dr. Jon Swift, Dean of St. Patrick's, Dublin,* was buried in the Churchyard of St. Andrew's, Northborough, Northampton.

Appendix II: The Family Petition to the House of Lords (1711-12)

To the Right Hon.*ble* the Lords Spiritual & Temporal in Parliam^{t}. Assembled.

The humble Petition of Hester Vanhomrigh widow and relict of Bartholomew Vanhomrigh late of the City of Dublin Esqr and Hester Vanhomrigh their daughter and Bartholomew and Mary Vanhomrigh Infants by their said Mother their guardian. Sheweth

That your Petitioners Husband and Father Bartholmew Vanhomrigh deced Did by his last Will & Testament bearing date the 2nd day of June 1701 Give and Devise That all his Lands Tenements Chattles Real and Personal Goods of all kind of Worldly Substance that he had or should have or be Intituled unto at the time of his death should within two Months after his decease be Inventoried valued and appraised (and after his debts and ffuneral charges satisfied) should be divided into so many equal parts as he should have children living att the time of his death and one part more to be put out to Interest, which Interest he did thereby direct to be paid to your Pet^{r}. Hester his wife dureing her Life, with other Devises over and made his said Wife Hester, John Pearson and Peter Partington Executors and Overseers as in and by the said Will may more fully appear.

Your Pet^{rs}. further shew that the said Devisor dyed sometime after making his said Will leaving the said Hester his widow the said Hester and Mary his two daughters and Ginkell and Bartholomew his two sons all under the age of 21

Richard Hawkins May ye 27th

Thomas Bacon October ye 27th

Thomas Son of Thomas & Pearsy Bolsho
December ye 1st.

Allemaford Nov. ye 14th

Tho. Swift Bro. to Dr. Jon. Swift
Dean of St. Patrick's Dublin. Decr. 3d.

1738

Will. S. of Richard and Habbaka
ngton April the 8th

James S. of John and Sarah Summer
July ye 2d.

PLATE III

The burial entry of Thomas Swift in the Register of Saint Andrew's Church Northborough, England.

years and that the Will was afterwards Established by Decree in the High Court of Chancery in Ireland as by the said Decree relation being thereunto had may appear

That the said Ginkell is since dead under the age of 21 years and Hester the daughter is now come to age, and in prospect of marriage but cannot receive her portion by reason the said Bartholomew her Brother being only of the Age of 19 years cannot sell any part of the Devised premises without the aid of an Act of Parliament.

That the said Peter Partington hath ever since the death of the said Devisor taken upon himself the Mannagement of the said Estate which being dispersed in severall Counties in Ireland and all the Petitioners living in this Kingdom are desireous to sell and dispose of the said Estate so left to them, and bring the produce thereof into this Kingdom which will tend very much to the advantage of your Petitioners.

Therefore your Petitioners humbly pray your Lordships to permit them to bring in a Bill to vest the lands tenements and hereditaments of which the said Devisor died seized in Trustees and their heirs to be sold and that the purchase money to be gott for the same may be divided into five equal parts, one part whereof to be enjoyed by the said Hester the Widow dureing her life with power to dispose of ffive hundred pounds thereof as by the said Will directed, and the other four parts together with what shall remain of the said fifth part after the decease of the said Hester the Widow to be equally divided between the other Petitioners the Children of the said Bartholomew Vanhomrigh.

And your Petrs. shall ever pray etc.

E. Van Homrigh
E. Van Homrigh
B. Van Homrigh
Mary Van Homrigh

Appendix III: The opinion of the Judges on the Family Petition (1711-12)

To the Right Hono: ble the Lords Spiritual and Temporal in Parliament Assembled

May it please Your Lordships

In pursuance of Yr Lordship's Order, bearing date the 22nd of January last past hereunto annext We have considered of the Bill therein mencioned and hereunto annext and considered of the matters refer'd do find the state of the Case to be as followeth Viz:

That Bartholomew Vanhomrigh late of the City of Dublin in the Kingdom of Ireland Esqr deceased by his last Will and Testament in Writeing bearing date the second day of June in the Year of Our Lord 1701 did Will and Devise that all his Lands and Tenements Chattles Real and Personal Debts due to him Money Plate Jewells Household goods and furniture living Cattle Corn and all and every kind of Worldly Substance whatsoever which he had or were Intituled to at the time of his death should be Inventoried Valued and appraised (and after his Debts and funeral charges satisfied) the remainder thereof according to such Valluation should be divided into so many equal parts as he should have Children living at the time of his Decease and one part more that is if he had 4 Children living at his Death his said Estate to be divided into five parts and if had five Children at the time of his Death the same to be divided into six parts and so more or less according to the Number of his Children so as there be always One part more than he should have Children at the time of his Death and that the Vallue in money of one part or Division of the said Estate Real and personal so vallued and divided should be put out at Interest which Interest he did thereby direct to be paid half Yearly to his Wife Hester during her life for her support and maintenance with a power to dispose of £500 out of the same at the time of her Decease and made his said Wife Hester during her Widowhood John Pierson and Peter Partinton Executors and Overseers of his said Will.

That the said Bartholomew Vanhomrigh some time after the making of his Will dyed leaving the said Hester his Widow Hester and Mary his two daughters and Bartholomew and Ginkell his two sons all under the age of one and twenty years. That the said Ginkell is since dead under the age of one and twenty years intestate and not marryed that Hester the Daughter has attained the age of one and twenty years But the said Bartholomew the brother being but of the age of nineteen years and the said Mary the sister of fifteen years, no part of the Lands and Tenements and Hereditaments which their said father dyed seized of can be sold without the aid of an Act of Parliament.

That the Premises lye disposed in several Counties in the Kingdom of Ireland and all Parties concerned in Interest in the same are now residing and intend to make their residence in England and are desireous that the said Premises be sold and the produce thereof brought into this Kingdome which will be more beneficial for all the Parties concerned therein than where the same now lies dispersed and remote from them

That the said Will was proved in Ireland (but by reason of the danger of the Seas) the parties concerned could not safely produce the Originall Will but only a probate thereof under the Seale of the Prerogative Court there whereas the Original Will ought to be produced and proved.

And we further certifie that the said Hester the Mother Bartholomew Hester and Mary the Son and Daughters acknowledged their hands to the Peticion and gave their Consents to the Bill hereunto annext and the said Hester the Mother and guardian of the said Son and Daughter Bartholomew and Mary consented also for them and the said John Pierson and Peter Partinton the Trustees and Executors in the said Will being in Ireland and not able to appear before Us proof was made of their consents to the said Bill under their hands and Seals by two Witnesses sworn at Your Lordships Bar. And there appears to be no other Parties concerned in the Consequences of the said Bill and that the Sale of the said Esate in Ireland will redound very much to the advantage of the Petitioners.

Wherefore We are humbly of Opinion It will be for the advantage of all parties concerned in the premisses if the Bill annext do pass into an Act which Bill we have perused and signed

All which We humbly submit to Your Lordships Consideration

Signed

ROBERT PRICE
ROBERT DORMER

Appendix IV: The Will of Mrs. Van Homrigh (1713-14)

In the Name of God Amen

I Hester Vanhomrigh of the Parish of St. James's Westminister in the County of Middlesex Widow Relict of Bartholomew Vanhomrigh late of Dublin in the Kingdom of Ireland Esq being sick and weak in body but praise be God for it of sound and disposing mind and memory do make and ordain this my last Will and Testament in manner and form following That is ffirst and principally I recommend my Soul into the hands of Almighty God that gave it And my body do remitt to the Earth to be buried in a decent but very private manner at the discretion of my Executrix thereinafter named And as for such wordly Estate as it hath pleased God to bless me with and which I have disposal of I do give desire and bequeath the same as is hereinafter mencioned Viz: ffirst I will and desire that all my proper and just debts which I shall owe at the time of my decease be paid and satisfied as soon as conveniently may be And I do give and bequeath unto my loving Son Bartholomew Vanhomrigh my silver dressing plate gold seal and large silver medal And unto my loving daughter Hester Vanhomrigh my diamond ear-rings and necklace and one pair of my silver candlesticks with my silver Snuffers and Snuff pan and my wedding Ring and Ruby ring with diamonds between and my furr-Tippett And unto my loving daughter Mary Vanhomrigh my pearl necklace and Ear-rings and the other pair of my silver candlesticks and my cornelian Ring with one diamond Also my Will is that my two small enamelled pictures and all my lockets shall be divided into two parts of equal value as near as may be and I do give one of the parts thereof unto my said daughter Hester Vanhomrigh and the other part thereof unto my said daughter Mary Vanhomrigh And my intencion and desire is that the same being so equally divided as aforesaid my said daughter Hester shall have the liberty of choosing which of the said two parts she shall think fitt Also I do give and bequeath unto my good friends Mr. John Pierson and Mr. Peter Partinton both of the said City of Dublin the sume of Ten Pounds apiece to buy them mourning Also I do give and bequeath unto Mary Whitlock my servant (if she shall be living with me at the time of my decease) all my wearing cloaths of silk linnen and woollen which shall have been worn by me And whereas my said husband Bartholomew Vanhomrigh in and by his last Will and Testament in writing bearing date the second day of June one thousand seven hundred and one did (amongst other things) will and bequeath that I might at my death by my Will attested by three or more credible witnesses dispose of the sum of five hundred pounds sterling to any ffriend of ffriends use or uses out of such part or share of his Estate as is therein for that purpose mencioned as by the said Will of my said late husband may more at large appear Now I do by this my last Will and Testament (executed in the presents of and attested by three or more credible Witnesses) give devise and dispose of the said sume of ffive hundred pounds and all and every sume and sums of money and all benefitt and advantage of or belonging unto me or at my disposal by vertue of the said Will of my said late Husband or of a late Act of Parliament for vesting the Estate of my said late Husband in Trustees or otherwise out of his Estate And also all the Rest and residue of my ready Money Securities for money Plate Jewells Goods Chattles and personal Estate whatsoever and wheresoever (my said debts Legacies and ffuneral charges being paid) unto my said son Bartholomew Vanhomrigh and my said daughters Hester Vanhomrigh and Mary Vanhomrigh their heirs Executors and Administrators respectively equally to be divided between them share and share alike. And I do hereby make constitute and appoint my said daughter Hester Vanhomrigh full and sole Executrix of this my last Will and Testament And I do hereby revoke and make void all former and other Wills and Testaments by me at any time heretofore made either in Word or Writing and do declare this to be my last Will and Testament In witness thereof I the said Hester Vanhomrigh have hereunto set my hand and seal this sixteenth day of January 1713 and in the Twelfth year of the

Reign of our Soveraign Lady Queen Anne over Great Britain E. Van Homrigh (signed and sealed)
Published and declared by the said Testatrix Hester Vanhomrigh for and as her last Will and Testament in the presence of us (who attest the same by subscribing our names in the presence of her the said Testatrix)

John White Henry White Thos. Bacon

Mrs. Van Homrigh's will was put into probate on the 11th February 1713-14.

Appendix V: Will of Bartholomew Van Homrigh Jnr. (1715)

In the name of God Amen.
I Bartholomew Van Homrigh of St. James's Westminister in the County of Middlesex Gent (only surviving son of Bartholomew Van Homrigh late of the City of Dublin in the Kingdom of Ireland Esq. deceased) being in good health of body and of sound and disposing mind and memory praise be God for it and considering the certainty of Death and the uncertainty of the time when it may happen to me make and ordaine this my Last Will and Testament in manner and forme following that is to say ffirst and principally I recommend my Soul into the hands of God that gave it and my body I commit to the earth to be decently buried att the discretion of my Executors hereinafter named and my Will and desire is that in case I shall happen to dye in Ireland that then my body be interred in the Parish Church of St. Andrews in the City of Dublin as near the body of my said Late ffather as conveniently may be and if I shall happen to dye

in Great Britain that then my body be interred in the parish Church of St. James's Westminster aforesaid as near as conveniently may be to the body's of my late deceased Mother and Brother and as for such Worldly Estate as it hath pleased God to bless me withall I do give devise and bequeath the same as hereinafter is mentioned. Whereas by the Last Will and Testament in writing of my said Late ffather bearing date the second day of June one thousand seven hundred and one all his Estate both reall and personall which he had or was intituled unto at the time of his Death was willed and devised to be valued and appraised and after payment of his Debts ffuneral and other charges the Remainder thereof was to be divided amongst and had and received by my said Late Mother and Brother (both since deceased) and my sisters and myself in the several parts shares and proportions and in the manner therein mentioned and whereas by an Act of Parliament made in or about the Eleventh year of her present Majestie's Reigne for vesting of my said late ffather's Estate in Ireland in Trustees to be sold all and singular the Lands and Tenements and hereditaments which my said late ffather or any other person or persons in Trust for him or to his use was seized or possessed of at the time of his Death were and are invested in John Peirson and Peter Partington therein named their Heirs Executors and Administrators respectively in Trust to sell and dispose of the same and to divide the moneys arising thereby and the profitts thereof according to the said Last Will and Testament of my said late ffather and the said Act of Parliament may now at large appear. Now my Will and Desire is that the said Estates of my said Late ffather and Premises or all my Parts Shares and proportions Right Title and Interest in or unto the same or any part thereof be sold and disposed of by the said John Peirson and Peter Partington their Heirs or Administrators respectively to the best Purchaser or Purchasers that can be gotten for the same and be converted into ready money as soon as may be after my decease and that all such summes of money as my late Mother did advance pay or disburse unto or for me or for my share of House-keeping Dyett Lodging and Travelling Charges in Equal proportion with her and with my said Brother and Sisters as have dwelt with her from time to time and all other just debts as I shall owe at the time of my decease be thereout and out of the Proffits untill such Sale or Sales paid and satisfyed in the ffirst place and I do give and bequeath unto the Reverend Doctor Benjamin Pratt Provost of Dublin Coledge in the said Kingdom of Ireland and Peter Partington of the said City of Dublin Gent the Summe of ffifty pounds a peice of Lawful Money of Great Britain also I doe give and bequeath unto Bartholomew Partington son of the said Peter Partington and unto John Hookes of Gaunts in the County of Dorsett and unto Erasmus Lewis Esq. the summe of ffifty pounds apeice of like money to buy them Mourning And unto the Reverend Mr. Periam Rector of Wimerton in the County of Wilts (heretofore my Tutor att Christchurch Colledge in Oxford) the Summe of thirty pounds of like Money to buy him Mourning And unto Mr. Thomas Bacon of the Middle Temple London the summe of Twenty pounds of like money to buy him Mourning And all the Rest and Residue of the moneys which shall be raised by such Sale or Sales as aforesaid and of the Rents and profitt until the makeing the same and whatsoever doth or shall belong unto me by virtue of the said Last Will and Testament of my said late ffather or the said Act of Parliament or either of them and of all other my Goods Chattells and personal Estate whatsoever and wheresoever not hereby otherwise disposed of after payment of my Debts ffuneral and other charges I doe give devise and bequeath unto the said Doctor Pratt and Peter Partington their Executors and Administrators upon Trust and Confidence Nevertheless and to and for the Intents and purposes hereinafter mentioned that is to say upon Trust and my Will is that they the said Doctor Pratt and Peter Partington their Executors Administrators doe and shall from time to time as any considerable part thereof shall come to their hands place the same out at Interest upon such Security as he or they shall be advised and conceive to be good and sufficient or otherwise secure and dispose of the same so as the greatest Interest proffits or Advantage may be made thereof that conveniently may be and doe and shall pay the Interest Produce or proffits thereof from time to time as the same shall arise or become due can be gotten in or received by them unto my loving sisters Esther Van Homrigh and Mary Van Homrigh equally to be divided Share and Share alike dureing the terme of their natural Lives and from and after the Death of either of my said Sisters then to the Survivor of them during the terme of her natural life And from and after the Death of the Survivor of my said Sisters my desire is that the said Bartholomew Partington son of the said Peter Partington and Godson of my said ffather if he shall be then living or otherwise the Heir male of his body Lawfully begotten do and shall take upon him and be constantly written and called by the Surname of Van Homrigh and in case he the said Bartholomew Partington if living or otherwise the Heir male of his body then living shall think fitting soe to doe then my Will and Mind is and I doe direct that as soon as may be after the Death of the survivor of my two said Sisters the said Doctor Benjamin Pratt and Peter Partington or the Survivor of them or the Executors or Administrators of such Survivor doe and shall (with the approbation of the said Bartholomew or in case of his Death of the Heir male of his body) by and with the said Rest and Residue of the Moneys to be raised by such Sale or Sales aforesaid and of my Goods and Chattells and personal Estate (after payment of my Debts Legacys and ffuneral and other Charges) Purchase a

Messuage or Messuages Lands Tenements and Hereditaments of Inheritance of as great yearly Value as may be had and purchased with the same and that the said Lands Tenements and Hereditaments so to be purchased therewith be settled and conveyed in the manner hereinafter mentioned (that is to say) to the use of the said Bartholomew for the terme of ninety-nine years if he shall so long live without impeachment of Wast and to Trustees and their Heirs during the Life of the said Bartholomew for preserving of the contingent Estates thereof from being barred and from and after his Death to the use of ffirst second third ffourth and all and every other son and sons of the Body of the said Bartholomew Lawfully Issuing severally and successively in Taile male The elder of such Son and Sons and the Heires Male of his body Issuing provided that the said Bartholomew and all and every person and persons who shall be intituled to the Estate to be purchased as aforesaid doe, always take upon them or beare and be constantly written and called by the Sirname of Van Homrigh my Intention and Desire being that the Estate soe to be purchased shall be enjoyed forever by a person of that Name But in case the said Bartholomew Partington at his Death shall leave no Issue Male of his body Lawfully begotten or if the said Bartholomew or his Heir Male or any other person who by virtue or in pursuance of this my Will shall become intituled to the Estate so to be purchased as aforesaid shall refuse to take or be written or called by the Sirname of Van Homrigh then my Will is that from and after the Death of the Survivor of my said Sisters and of the said Bartholomew without Issue Male of his body surviving or from and after such refusal of taking the said Name of Van Homrigh as aforesaid which shall first happen respectively then the said Doctor Benjamin Pratt and Peter Partington or the Survivor of them or the Executors or Administrators of such survivor doe and shall pay all the rest and residue of the moneys to be raised by such Sale or Sales as aforesaid and of my said personal Estate or Assigne and convey the Securities for the same if not laid out in the Such Purchase as aforesaid, or if such Purchase be made that the Estate so purchased shall be sold and the Money raised thereby with the Proffits till Sale shall be paid to Dublin Colledge in the said Kingdom of Ireland and shall be appropriated applyed and disposed of on and for the Erecting and finishing of some convenient Building, of use in or adjoining to and for the benefitt of the said last mentioned Colledge and not otherwise and that the Building soe to be erected therewith shall forever beare or be called by the name of Van Homrigh and I doe hereby make constitute and appoint the said Doctor Benjamin Pratt and Peter Partington Executors of this my Last Will and Testament and Earnestly Intreat them to see the same duly performed to the utmost of their power and for their care and paines therein I doe give and bequeath unto each of them (besides what I have hereinbefore given to them) the Summe of ffifty pounds apeice to be had and received by them, as soon as may be after they respectively shall prove this my Will and take upon them the Trusts hereby reposed in them Provided always nevertheless and for the Encouragement of my said Executors and Trustees to act in the Executorshipp and Trusts my Will and meaning is that it shall and may be Lawfull to and for the said Doctor Pratt and Peter Partington their Executors and Administrators from time to time in the first place to deduct detaine and satisfye unto themselves out of what shall come to their hands by virtue hereof all such reasonable Charges Costs and Expences as they respectively shall expend or sustaine or be put unto in the performance or execution of this my Will or the Trusts hereby reposed in them or in anywise touching or concerning the same and that they shall not be answerable for or chargeable with more of my said Estate than shall actually come to their hands respectively nor for any Involuntary Losses or Losses which shall or may happen without his or their owne willfull Default respectively nor one of them for the Receipts Payments Acts or Doeings of the other of them But each of them respectively for his owne Receipts Payments Acts and Doeings only anything herein before contained to the contrary thereof not withstanding.

In witness I the said Bartholomew Van Homrigh have put unto this my Last Will and Testament Comprized or Written in six sheets of paper and part of the seventh sheet att the Topp thereof sett my Seale this third day of March Anno Domini 1713 and the twelfth year of the Reigne of Our Soveraigne Lady Anne by the Grace of God of Great Britain France and Ireland Queen Defender of the ffaith (B. Van Homrigh) Signed sealed published and declared by the said Testator Bartholomew Van Homrigh for and as his Last Will and Testament in the presence of us (who attest the same by subscribing our names in the presence of him the said Testator

Ri Tanner William Lingard John Turner

Put into Probate 17th May 1715.

Appendix VI: The Will of Mrs. Jane Fenton (1735–6)

In the name of God Amen I Jane Fenton of Guldesford in the County of Surrey Widow do make my Last Will and Testament in manner and form following First I Commend my soul to God hoping to be saved by the death of Jesus Christ and I order my body to be decently buryed and as concerning my Worldly Estate I give and dispose thereof as followeth to wit I give and bequeath unto Alice Fenton daughter of my late husband Joseph Fenton deceased by his first wife my gold watch also I give and bequeath to Richard Fenton son of my said late husband by his first wife my silver hand candlestick and snuffers and to Anne his wife my silver Cann Also I give and release to my son-in-law Jonathan Jackson all money that shall be due and owing from him to me at the time of my decease Also I give and bequeath to my granddaughter Jane Jackson all my linnen of all sorts and all my wearing apparell to be delivered to her at her age of one and twenty years or day of Marriage which shall first happen and in case of her death before such time then give the same to the said Richard Fenton Also I give and bequeath unto Mrs. Mose now or late of Farnham Mrs. Swift of Puttenham and Mrs. Hewatson of Dublin if she be living if not to her husband one guinea apiece to buy them rings Also I give and bequeath the sum of ten pounds to be applied to such charitable uses as my Executors hereinafter named shall think fit Also I give and bequeath to the Reverend Mr. Bannister of Guldeford or whom else shall preach a funeral sermon for me two guineas. Also I give and bequeath to William Herswell of Guldeford aforesaid Mealman the sum of ten pounds in case he shall accept of the trust hereinafter by me reposed in him Also I give and bequeath unto the said Richard Fenton and William Herswell all the rest and residue of my Goods Chattells rights Credits ready money and personal estate whatsoever (after my debts and funeral expenses paid and discharged) in trust to pay and apply the yearly income interests and profits that can be made thereof towardes the maintenance education and bringing up of my said granddaughter Jane Jackson until her age of one and twenty years or day of Marriage which shall first happen and then to pay her thereout the sum of one hundred pounds of lawful money of Great Britain And from thenceforth I will that the said Richard Fenton shall have the yearly income interest and profits that can be made of the residue thereof during his natural life for his own use and property and at his decease I will the said residue thereof to be paid to my said Granddaughter Jane Jackson her executors or administrators But in case she shall happen to dye before she shall attain the age of one and twenty years or be marryed then and from thenceforth I will and bequeath all the said rest and residue of my said goods Chattells rights credits ready money and Personal Estate to the said Richard Fenton his executors and administrators for his and their own property But in such case I will he or they shall pay ten pounds thereout to his sister Alice Fenton her executors or administrators and I nominate and appoint the said Richard Fenton and William Herswell to be joynt executors of this my last Will and Testament And my further will and meaning is that neither of my said Trustees and Executors shall be charged or chargeable with or for any part of my estate further or otherwise than only for such and so much thereof as shall come to each of their respective hands and disposals And in case any moneys shall happen to be lost by being put out on bad security or otherwise that my said trustees and executors or either of them shall not be charged or chargeable with or answerable for the same And I revoke all Wills by me made In testimony whereof I have hereto set my hand and seal the eight and twentyth day of February in the seventh year of the Reign of King George the Second of Great Britain and so forth and in the year of Our Lord one thousand seven hundred thirty and three Jane Fenton Signed sealed published and declared by the said Jane Fenton to be her last Will and Testament in the presence of us. Humphrey Harrison. John Shotter.

Put into Probate 8th March 1735-6.

Appendix VII: Vanessa's Will

In the name of God, Amen. I Esther Vanhomrigh, one of the daughters of Bartholomew Vanhomrigh, late of the City of Dublin, Esq., deceased, being of sound and disposing mind and memory, do make and ordain this my last will and testament, in manner and form following, that is to say:—First, I recommend my soul into the hands of Almighty God, and my body I commit to the earth, to be buried at the discretion of my executors hereinafter named. In the next place, I give and devise all my worldly substance, whether in lands, tenements, hereditaments or trusts, and all my real and personal estate, of what nature or kind soever, unto the Reverend Doctor George Berkly, one of the fellows of Trinity College, Dublin, and Robert Marshall of Clonmell, Esq., their heirs, executors and administrators, chargeable nevertheless with, and subject and liable to the payment of all such debts of my own contracting, as I shall owe at the time of my death, as also unto the payment of the several legacies hereinafter bequeathed, or which shall hereafter be bequeathed by an codicil to be attached to this my last will and testament: *Item*, I give and bequeath to Erasmus Lewis of London, Esq., the sum of twenty-five pounds sterling, to buy a ring: *Item*, I give and bequeath to Francis Annesley of the city of London, Esq., twenty-five pounds sterling, to buy a ring: *Item*, I give and bequeath to John Hooks, Esq., of Gaunts in Dorsetshire, twenty-five pounds sterling, to buy a ring: *Item*, I give unto the Right Reverend Father in God, William King, Lord Archbishop of Dublin, twenty-five pounds sterling, to buy a ring: *Item*, I give and bequeath unto the Right Reverend Father in God, Theop. Bolton, Lord Archbishop of Clonfert, twenty-five pounds sterling, to buy a ring: *Item*, I give and bequeath unto Robert Lindsey, of the city of Dublin, Esq., twenty-five pounds sterling, to buy a ring: *Item,* I give and bequeath unto Edmund Shuldam of the City of Dublin, Esq., twenty-five pounds sterling, to buy a ring; *Item,* I give and bequeath unto William Lingin of the Castle of Dublin, Esq., twenty-five pounds sterling, to buy a ring; *Item,* I give and bequeath unto the Rev. Mr. John Antrobus, my cousin, the like sum of money, to buy a ring: *Item,* I give and bequeath unto Bryan Robinson, doctor of physic in the City of Dublin, fifteen pounds sterling, to buy a ring: *Item,* I give and bequeath unto Mr. Edward Cloker of the City of Dublin, fifteen pounds sterling, to buy a ring: *Item,* I give and bequeath to Mr. William Marshall of the city of Dublin, fifteen pounds sterling, to buy a ring: *Item,* I give and bequeath to John Finey, son of George Finey of Kildrought in the county of Kildare, and godson to my sister, the sum of twenty-five pounds sterling, to be paid him when he shall attain the age of twenty-one years: Also I give and bequeath to his mother, Mrs. Mary Finey, the sum of ten pounds sterling, to buy mourning; and to Mrs. Ann Wakefield, her sister, of the parish of St. Andrews in the city of Dublin, the like sum, to buy mourning: *Item,* I give and bequeath unto Ann Kindon, who is now my servant, the sum of twenty-five pounds sterling, to buy mourning; and to her daughter, Ann Clinkskells, the like sum of money, to buy mourning: *Item,* I give and bequeath unto every servant that shall live with me at the time of my death half a year's wages; and to the poor of the parish, where I shall happen to die, five pounds sterling: And I do hereby make, constitute and appoint the said Dr. George Berkly, and Robert Marshall, Esq., of Clonmel, sole executors of this my last will and testament: And I do hereby revoke and make void all former and other wills and testaments by me in any wise heretofore made, either in word or writing, and declare this to be my last will and testament. In witness whereof I, the said Esther Vanhomrigh, have hereunto set my hand and seal, this first day of May, in the year of Our Lord 1723.

E. Van Homrigh. (Seal)

Signed, published and declared by the said Esther Vanhomrigh, for and as her last will and testament, in presence of us, who attest the same by subscribing our names in the presence of her the said testatrix.

Jas. Doyle. Ed. Thrush. Darby Gafny.

The last will and testament of Esther Vanhomrigh, late deceased (having, and so forth), was proved in common form of law, and probate granted by the most Reverend Father in God Thomas, and so forth, to the Reverend George Berkely and Robert Marshall, the executors, they being first sworn personally.

Dated the 6th day of June, 1723.

A true copy, which I attest.

John Hawkins, Dep. Reg.

Appendix VIII: Swift's membership of Freemasonry

The important fact that Dean Swift was a Freemason has not been taken into consideration by editors of his work, some of which requires an understanding of Freemasonic ceremonies and symbolism.

There is no existing record of Swift's having been a member of any Irish Lodge, but, according to information kindly supplied by the Grand Lodge, London, in a letter dated 8-XII-59, he was a member of a Lodge

which was granted Warrant No. 16, on 3rd April 1723, to meet at the Red Lion, Tottenham Court Road, London. In 1729, the Lodge moved to The Goat, at the foot of the Haymarket. It was erased from the List of Lodges on 21st November 1745. The Grand Lodge minute book, under heading List of the Names of the Members of all the regular Lodges, as they were returned in the year 1730, *records the name of Jonathan Swift as a member of the Lodge meeting at The Goat, at the foot of the Haymarket: The date of initiation is not shown, but the Dean is known to have been in London in 1726 and 1727 as the guest of Pope, and it is probable that he became a Mason during that time.*

Not only Alexander Pope, but also Swift's other close friend, Dr. Arbuthnot, was a member of that Lodge.

Although there is not any existing record that Swift belonged to an Irish Lodge, many of his friends did, and in the Dean's opposition to *Mr. Wood's Halfpence*, he was given invaluable support by Irish Freemasonry.

It is not known what Degree was reached by Dean Swift, so it cannot be asserted that he was a Member of The Royal Arch. According to F. de P. Castell's *Antiquity of the Holy Royal Arch*, this Degree of Masonry existed prior to 1723. But, during Swift's last, terrible phase of mental decay, his household reported that the old man used to repeat, *I am what I am . . . . . I am what I am . . . .*

A very slight alteration in those words would suggest that, in his last fearful ordeal, a Member of the Royal Arch Degree was calling for help.

Appendix IX: Swift and Vanessa

Chapter III; paragraph 5.

Since the available evidence would seem to show that this poem was written for Esther Van Homrigh *before* Swift became a dean, the use of the anagram *Cadenus* for *Decanus* has caused a great deal of speculation. A possible explanation may be that this name—specially invented by Swift for intimate use between himself and the girl for whom he also invented the name Vanessa—had a totally different derivation. The Oxford Dictionary gives a XVII Century meaning of the word *Cad*, as *a familiar spirit*, and quotes two extracts from writers of that period, in which the word is so used. Swift's handwriting was not always very legible, and his *V* might have been easily misread as U by a stranger. If this mistake had been made, their secret name may, in reality, have been an anagram of *Cad Es Vn* i.e. *The familiar spirit of Esther Van (Homrigh)*. Several times in their letters allusions are made to witchcraft; Swift constantly used diminutives of *Esther*, and in his *Journal to Stella* he habitually referred to her family as the *Vans*.

After Vanessa's death, the poem was found among her papers, and copies were surreptiously distributed in Dublin. The name would, very reasonably, have been taken to be an anagram of *Decanus*, Swift being then long a dean. Some years later, Swift would have accepted the happy alteration, when he himself edited the poem.

Vanessa's use of the name *Cad*, in her letters to Swift, would be very much more significant if the XVII Century meaning of the word were accepted instead of its being a somewhat clumsy abbreviation.

Bibliography

The following is a list of the chief sources which have been consulted.

The Works of the Rev. Jonathan Swift D.D. edited by John Hawkesworth. London 1755.
The Words of the Rev. Jonathan Swift, D.D. arranged by

Thomas Sheridan, A.M., revised by John Nichols, F.S.A., London 1808.
Remarks on the Life and Writings of Dr. Jonathan Swift, by John, Earl of Orrery. Dublin 1752.
Observations upon Lord Orrerys Remarks, by Dr. Delaney 1754.
Essay upon the Life, Writings and Character of Dr. Swift, by Deane Swift. 1755.
The Life of the Revd. Jonathan Swift, Hawkesworth, 1755.
Letters written by the late Dr. Jonathan Swift, Dean of St. Patrick's, Dublin. Published from the originals collected and revised by Deane Swift. Dublin 1768.
The Drapier Letters. Faulkner, Dublin. 1762.
The Life of the Rev. Dr. Jonathan Swift. T. Sheridan 1784.
Enquiry into the Life of Dean Swift. George Monck Berkeley 1789.
Literary Relics. George Monck Berkeley 1789.
The Diary of John Evelyn, edited by Austin Dobson. Macmillan 1908.
Memoirs of Mrs. Letitia Pilkington - 1748. George Routledge & Sons, London 1928.
History and Antiquities of the Collegiate Church of St. Patrick, W. Monck Mason 1820.
The Correspondence of Jonathan Swift D.D., edited by F. Elrington Ball, G. Bell & Sons, London, 1910.
The Poems of Jonathan Swift, edited by Harold Williams, Clarendon Press, Oxford, 1937.
Journal to Stella, edited by Harold Williams, Clarendon Press, Oxford, 1948.
Gulliver's Travels, edited by Harold Williams, London.
Vanessa and her Correspondence with Jonathan Swift, edited by A. Martin Freeman, London 1921.
Jonathan Swift, a critical essay, W. D. Taylor 1933.
The Closing Years of Dean Swift's Life. Sir W. Wilde 1849

The Life of Jonathan Swift. Sir Henry Craik. 1882.
The Life of Jonathan Swift. John Foster 1875
Jonathan Swift, a biographical and critical study, John Churton Collins 1893.
Swift. Sir Leslie Stephens. 1889
Swift or the Egoist. Rossi and Hone 1934
Swift. Carl Van Doren 1931
In Search of Swift. Denis Johnston, Dublin 1959
The Conjured Spirit. Evelyn Hardy. 1949.
Martha, Lady Giffard, Life and letters, Julia Longe 1911
Stella, a Gentlewoman of the Eighteenth Century, Herbert Davis 1942.
Swift's Marriage to Stella. Maxwell Gold. 1935
The Life and friendships of Dean Swift. Stephen Gwynn 1933
Dean Swift and his writings. G. P. Moriarty 1893
Jonathan Swift. J. Middleton Murry 1954
Betham's Geneological Abstracts, Records Office, Dublin.
Registers of St. Patrick's Cathedral, Dublin.
Calender of Ancient Records of Dublin, edited by J. T. Gilbert.
Dictionary of National Biography.
Publications of the Parish Register Society of Dublin.
Gentleman's Magazine, November, 1757
Foundation of the Hospital of King Charles II in Dublin. F. R. Falkiner.
Records of the House of Lords, London.
Parish Register of St. Andrew's Church, Northborough, England.
Parish Register of St. James's Church, London.
Principal Probate Registry, Somerset House, London.
Transcript of Northborough Parish Register, 1738
Antiquity of the Holy Royal Arch, F. deP. Castells, London 1927

Index

APPENDICES